# DAILY TELEGRAPH
# GUIDE TO EASIER GARDENING

**Daily Telegraph**

# GUIDE TO
# EASIER GARDENING

## VIOLET STEVENSON

Collins
London and Glasgow

Printed in Great Britain by
William Collins Sons & Co. Ltd.
London & Glasgow

First published 1978

© *Daily Telegraph*
ISBN 0 00 412085 X

# CONTENTS

# 1

## GARDENING IS WHAT YOU MAKE IT

Gardeners throughout the world can almost certainly be classified according to various well defined types. Look around at your friends and neighbours, consider your relatives and your visitors, and regard their attitudes to their gardens. You will probably find that the person's predisposition, his philosophy, his attitude to life matters more than the problems of his particular garden. By this I mean that the garden itself can be large or small, rural or urban, complex or simple, sophisticated or cottage-type, ornamental or food productive, yet the basic method of attack will be the same for people of the same general attitude to life.

There is the man who comes home from the office and cannot shed his formal clothes quickly enough to dress in elaborately bucolic and slightly raffish uniform, muddy and oil-stained. Out he goes to the garden with his wheelbarrow of tools and when he reaches the location of his intended task he reaches into his pocket, pulls out his pipe, lights it, and gazes about him in contentment. He will do very little creative work during his session in the garden, but he will enjoy himself, secure and happy in the knowledge that he is productive, virtuous, leading a healthy outdoor life, and contributing to the welfare not only of his own family but of the world as a whole.

Or there is a woman returning from some social affair who, having slipped into a comfortable dress or slacks to do a bit of gardening, is most likely to dead-head a few flowers while she dreams of seeds she will sow next year.

And what about the man who is a real whirlwind of energy? He almost runs down to his working site and his spade is in the soil almost before he has stopped running. Soil flies about in great, heavy clods. There is much thudding and banging, a good deal of stertorous breathing and gradually his complexion changes from a pale pink through to a blotchy purple. The purpose of the digging is of less

7

importance than the digging itself. Gardening is not so much a means of growing vegetables or flowers as an opportunity of exercising the muscles, working off excess energy, and possibly shedding some of the furies and frustrations of the commercial day.

He is probably married to the lady who dashes about mowing the lawn almost every day or sweeps the paths in a frenzy of cleanliness. Straight from dusting the house she dusts the garden, the purity mattering less than the purging.

Compare these with the perfectionist, the gardener who challenges you to find a single weed in his lawn, a single aphis on his roses. One of his tools is a tape measure and every bed, every border conforms in overall size and in the spacing of each plant to the theories to which he subscribes. His hedges seem to be made almost of stone, so regular are they. His paving never has a weed in any crack. His gravel is raked, his shrubs pruned to uniform size, his climbers carefully trained and tied in. His tools are cleaned and oil-wiped each time he finishes his work and his mower is sent for servicing in January each year. He cleans the windows of his tool shed, labels his tool racks, and his compost heap is a meticulous model of science and architecture.

Then there are the botanists, who will not grow a Russian vine but in its place put a *Polygonum baldschuanicum* – 'Or, with the modern nomenclature,' they laugh with deprecatory erudition, 'should it now be *Polygonum bilderdyckia baldschuanicum*?' They define their plants rather than admire or enjoy them. They will uproot a familiar species in favour of a rare one. It matters not that they garden on limestone, if they wish to include a calcifuge in their territory they will import acid soil, drench it in sequestrene, and insist that the plant grows.

How unlike our next type, usually male, who grows only for size. His sunflowers are the tallest, his pumpkins the heaviest, his onions the largest, leeks the thickest and whitest. He will dig four feet down to allow room for his carrots to develop. He will pinch out side shoots and buds until his single remaining chrysanthemum bloom rivals a football in circumference. He is constantly searching for fresh topsoil, or greensand. He mixes weird potions and there are always heaps of decomposing organic matter from land or sea dotted about his plot. He is ruthless with pest or disease, preferring where possible to kill the first with his finger and thumb and thorough enough with the second to dig up and burn a crop rather than attempt to cure its affliction.

And by contrast there are the tender-hearted gardeners who will gently brush a caterpillar off a rose and carry it guiltily to the fence, to be tipped into a neighbour's plot. They will talk to their plants to encourage them. They will flatter them shamelessly and consider that they do them a favour when they cut them to bring indoors for the further enjoyment of the family.

One could go on almost indefinitely. There is always the 'You should have seen it last week' or the 'Come and see it next week when it's at its best' type. And there's the meek 'My wife's the gardener, I'm just the odd job man,' and the loud and arrogant 'My father won every prize in the county with his leeks and what was good enough for him's good enough for me. Don't hold with these new-fangled methods.' And the 'Every bit of it natural, not a drop, not a grain of artificial chemicals. Never know what long-term damage they're going to do.'

And does it really matter? We can all of us be mad in our own particular pattern yet be perfectly intelligent and productive garden-ers. The types we have just been looking at are displaying their *attitudes* to gardening more than their actual activities. The man who hurls himself at his plot and the dilettante can both achieve much the same results without altering their fundamental outlooks. For basic-ally every gardener wishes to make his plot look good and be pro-ductive. He wants to enjoy its appearance, to know that it is a credit to him and to his neighbourhood, and to know at the same time that the quality and quantity of his flowers, his fruit, and his vegetables have given him a sound return on his investment and labour.

There is, I suggest, a further gardening virtue which too many of us tend to ignore, and that is looking to the future.

When a young couple move into their first home, statistics say that this will probably be an older property, not a newly built house. This is for the obvious reason that their finances at this stage will not reach to the higher price of the more modern building. With their older property they will probably find that the garden has already been made according to the wishes and needs of the previous occupant and they will set about altering it to suit their own needs. They are comparatively impecunious, but they are young, energetic, strong, ambitious, and determined to make the most of their plot. They will wish to make it pay for itself in the production of food, both to aid their finances and to improve their diet, for they are intelligent and progressive people.

They are now faced with the danger that in their looking ahead they will see only tomorrow, not next week. They make the major part of their plot into a productive allotment and then begin to run into problems. They find that they are growing more than they can immediately consume and yet they have no facilities for preserving the excess. They find that they are so committed to their vegetable garden that they cannot afford time off, that it comes into its greatest production at a time when they had hoped to take a holiday away from home. They find that it has become a chore, a liability, an activity to be avoided if possible. Then develops the guilty conscience which eventually induces a genuine dislike of gardening.

I would most strongly urge that the first thing to do with a new garden, any new garden, whether empty or filled, raw or mature, is to live with it for a while as it is, then to make it comfortable for you. Always complete your gardening in the areas nearest the house first, working outwards as time goes by. Make it as easy as possible to manage. Devise means of cutting down labour, of easing tasks, of avoiding irritations and frustrations.

To give just one simple example: a couple of days 'wasted' in easing the path to your garage, widening the entrance, smoothing the corner, paving the track, will in the long run save hours of time and vast quantities of nervous energy. In the first few weeks you will be bringing a considerable number of articles, some of them awkward in shape, to the new house, and ease of loading and unloading will be essential.

Again, if possible pave right round the house, leaving planting holes for climbers at strategic points. This will mean that at all times and in all weathers you will be able to walk around your home dry shod and with clean feet. And while you are doing this, why not extend the paving a little in one convenient spot and make a little paved terrace or patio? If it is laid efficiently it will never need further attention, so it will save much labour. It will also give you a tremendous moral boost, for there are few gardening pleasures more profound than sitting in sunny comfort to admire your work in progress. At the same time, you have the certain knowledge that you have improved your property significantly and added to its capital value.

If instead, on first purchase of the home you had hurried daily down to the end of the garden through all the mud and had there slaved to plant potatoes and cabbages to help the family budget, you would have returned eventually to the house tired, muddy, anxious, and dyspeptic, and you would have added nothing to the value of your home.

So the first lesson in successful gardening is to consider your own comfort and pleasure before anything else. 'People is more important than things' is a wise saying. Never take a garden too solemnly. Jolly it along. Get it on your side. Leave it to itself occasionally to manage as best it can, for this shows that you have faith and trust in its inherent native ability and sturdiness. Like a judo enthusiast, learn to benefit from your opponent's strength. If a corner of the garden appears to be wet and boggy, why go to all the trouble and expense of draining it? Instead build a pool and bog garden there.

Go along with the garden; don't always try to fight it. Yet never lose sight of the fact that on occasion the recalcitrant behaviour of some section or feature of the garden may very well be a cry for help, a sign of sickness, and be prepared to wade in with every weapon in your armoury to rescue the distressed. If you learn to work with your garden, treating it always as an equal with a legitimate life of its own, you will learn all the earlier the reasons behind the failure of this crop or the death of that tree. Make a partner of your garden and you have made a good working team.

Remember always that no garden is static. Once it has been designed and created it does not stay still and live forever in that stage. The plants develop, the trees grow, the shrubs spread and inevitably certain changes have to be made. But this is all to the good, for just as no garden is static, so no human being is, either. We all develop and change. Perhaps we become more prosperous and are able to carry out changes in the garden that hitherto were out of our reach. Perhaps children arrive or children depart, each event urging on us changes to adapt the garden to altered circumstances. And alas, perhaps illness, accident, or age make it imperative that our style of gardening is made simpler, easier, gentler, within the range of painful muscles or other restricted capability.

One of the essentials of good gardening is to strive towards making tasks easier, quicker, more productive, and this policy should look forward to the time when the garden is going to get too much for us. Gradually we find that certain tasks take much longer to complete than they used to do, or that some tasks seem always to be left undone because of a reluctance to embark on them. These are signs that somewhere something is wrong, and we should be able to read these signs and learn the message they have for us.

But this need not happen only to those who are getting elderly or infirm. It can happen to anyone. In our own garden many years ago we noticed that a certain portion of the grass, tucked away and somehow divorced from the major lawns, never seemed to get mown. This area tended to become unkempt and weedy. The longer the grass grew the more difficult it was to cut. Eventually we learnt our lesson: we were reluctant to mow the grass here because it was out of the way, it meant bringing the mower around behind a long flower bed. The grass ran from the back of this bed to a wild farm hedge which was constantly full of weeds and these weeds tended to grow into the grass. It was, in fact, a difficult area to mow, so it didn't get mown. It was that simple. The answer? Pave it. Once that was done we had no more trouble, the area looked neat at all times. It demanded no attention and we had more time to give to more important sections of the garden. And perhaps most important of all, our guilt was assuaged and our irritation relieved.

So any task that does not get carried out as often or as readily as it should is a sure indication that there is something wrong. Nearly always a recognition of this fact is sufficient and a remedy is quickly forthcoming. This way the plot *gradually* becomes easier and easier to handle and to keep under control, and the general result obtained is more effective than it would have been if the gardener had suddenly sat down one day with the intention of simplifying his gardening work and produced a series of drastic proposals to that end. Evolution is generally more satisfactory than revolution.

On the whole, however, it is probably necessary to live with a garden for a number of seasons before one begins to recognize its needs, and sometimes it becomes apparent that changes will have to be made before evolution can bring them gradually about. It is helpful in this connection to recognize that certain garden features demand more attention than others. An obvious example was the grassy area in our own garden referred to above. Once the considerable constructional task had been completed, we found that a paved area was easier to maintain than the same area covered in difficult grass.

Which takes more work, flower beds or vegetable patch? Which is more demanding in time, soft fruits or stone fruits? Which costs more to maintain, the ornamental pool or the rock garden? Is the greenhouse a help or a tie?

It is not always possible to be strictly objective when answering questions such as these, for our own preferences enter too closely into our replies. To take an example again, we could say that the total ground area of a greenhouse is almost exactly the same as the space occupied in the garden by the ornamental pool. You find that you spend twice as much time in the greenhouse as you do working with the pool. Naturally enough the pool is soon filled with decaying leaves and looks a mess, whereas the greenhouse is a real delight. So if a choice has to be made between one or the other, which will you select? The answer is surely that you enjoy working in the greenhouse and do not enjoy working with or in the pool, so the greenhouse wins in spite of the fact that it inevitably occupies more of your time.

Nevertheless, it is essential to examine the virtues and the drawbacks of certain garden features as objectively as possible, so that one can have a reliable basis for decisions about allocation of space, time, labour, and even money in the garden. This we attempt to do in the next chapter.

# 2

## WHERE THE HARD WORK LIES

As with every aspect of life, so every aspect of gardening has its advantages and its disadvantages. One can imagine the delight of sipping a cool drink beside a tropical pool when the sun has set and the light breeze just riffles the water. But one prefers not to think of the humming hordes of mosquitoes that explore every inch of bare flesh. Equally, one imagines with delight the flavour of sun-warmed strawberries straight from the plot into the dish, and forgets the spraying, the layering, the strawing, the protecting, and even the picking.

But some kinds of gardening do make lesser demands than others. The most obvious way of creating a truly labour-saving garden would be to pave over the entire area, and there are conditions under which this extreme answer would be the wise and correct one. This would be where the plot is small, urban, overshadowed and has thin, poor, sour soil. With these limitations, probably the only means of making a useful and attractive garden would be to pave the entire area and then install tubs, pots, troughs, and similar containers, which could be moved around the plot to follow the light and could be continuously replenished with fresh materials as is necessary, to provide a constant reminder of growing things, a constant suggestion of green and flower colour, and to furnish the walls with plants.

It might appear here that the first considerable labour and the first considerable cost would be the last; but not so. Containers have to be constantly replenished with fresh materials, not a very onerous task but possibly expensive. They will also demand very frequent watering if their soil is not to dry out and the plants die. But overall this is a labour-saving type of garden, of which only a comparatively small number of examples are normally to be seen in this country except in the centre of major cities.

## The Lawn

Let us now look in some detail at the most popular features of average small gardens to see what advantages they may hold for us and what drawbacks, and let us begin with lawns, because almost every garden has a lawn of some kind, large or small, even though it may be sometimes out of character. It might be imagined that a lawn will require little expenditure of time, money or labour once it has been established. Let us ignore the major task and the major cost of first laying the lawn and concentrate on its maintenance in a reasonable condition.

All lawns are made either of fine grasses or tougher, coarser, more utility grasses or a mixture of the two, but so long as they receive the use appropriate to the type of grass, there will be little to choose between them in the long run, except that the coarser grasses generally grow more quickly and will require more frequent mowing. Every lawn, coarse or fine, should be cut at least once a week during the growing season if it is to be called a lawn rather than a paddock or a meadow.

A coarse lawn can be cut by a coarse machine, that is, a rotary one with cutter bar or blades which revolve parallel to the ground and so slash the blades of grass, whereas the finer grasses making the finer lawn should have a more expensive and more refined machine with blades set into a drum or barrel, revolving and catching the grass between the blades and a cutter bar so that they are cut in a scissors action. There is no cheap, hand-propelled version of the former type because a machine of some kind is necessary to turn blades with sufficient speed to slash the grass efficiently.

There are many inexpensive kinds of powered machines, both rotary and cylinder, the least expensive powered by electricity, light, easy, starting at a touch and costing very little more than a hand-propelled model. They are suitable only for comparatively small areas and they require little maintenance. Larger areas of grass require larger, heavier, and considerably more expensive machines, costly to run and requiring regular and today astronomically expensive maintenance, unless you are capable of doing it yourself.

Lawns not only grow grass, they grow weeds. It is impossible to weed a lawn, however thoroughly, and know that it will remain weed-free for the entire season. A fine and carefully maintained lawn can be hand weeded, but for most of us the weeds are too numerous and we must rely on lawn sand or selective weedkillers to do our work for us. These are effective but they are expensive and they take considerable time and care to apply if we are not to suffer from burnt patches or untreated strips of grass.

Some lawns require drainage in the form of an annual spiking if they are to perform well, and others may need periodic levelling as bumps and hollows appear, generally from the activity of moles or mice below ground. Fungus attacks on some lawns require treatment.

But the major drawback to a lawn as a feature is still the necessary frequency of the mowing. A well-designed lawn, where the mower can be guided easily over the surface, may take a comparatively short time in the actual mowing. What takes the time and the energy is the emptying of the grassbox or the careful manoeuvring of the machine past shrubs, under trees, or through narrow, tortuous paths and into sharply angled corners. If the garden has more than one level it may be difficult to get a heavy machine to other parts, or if on a steep slope it may be difficult to mow at all.

So we might summarize the value of a lawn as a garden feature by saying that if the shape of the area is right, the slope is right, and the machine is right the labour required will not be excessive. Costs for a good lawn will always be comparatively high if you take into account the initial cost of a machine, the price of the fuel it uses, and the expense of regular maintenance or even occasional replacement.

This being so, why have a lawn? Partly because it is the accepted, the traditional thing in this country and partly because there is no doubt that the green we are so fortunate as to be able to enjoy is an admirable foil to all flower colours.

I have seen and admired a number of gardens with no lawn at all. One was a shingle or gravel garden. The flower beds were informal, scattered, large, and the space between them was covered with gravel. This would have been impossible not many years ago because the gravel would have required constant weeding. But today with modern weedkillers a single application once a year will keep the area free of all weeds.

Another garden without a lawn which I have much admired is somewhat smaller and composed entirely of a series of beds and borders surrounded by stone and separated by paved paths. In neither of these gardens is there any sense of loss from the lack of grass.

Some of the most ancient Japanese gardens were built without grass, using mainly sand or fine gravel to separate the various garden features. This surface was frequently raked or brushed into patterns to give it added interest and attraction.

## Flowers, Trees and Shrubs

The lawn then, or the gravel or sand or paved areas, serves mainly to set off and separate the various beds and borders, some with flowers, some with trees and shrubs, and some with a mixture of the two. Here the evaluation chart zigzags wildly up and down, for flower beds and borders can be among the most expensive features in the garden in terms of time and labour and perhaps even finance, whereas tree and shrub borders can be among the least expensive after the initial cost of purchasing and installing the plants.

The flowers can be annuals, biennials, or perennials, the first two types being highly expensive in labour but comparatively cheap on finance if they are raised from seed; they can be extremely colourful if this is what you wish. Most perennial plants require dividing every three or four years, a task which can involve considerable time and expenditure of energy. So long as the soil is kept in good heart and fed regularly, actual maintenance costs will be light except for the price of occasional replacement.

Most trees and shrubs, once planted correctly, will live almost without attention for many years, and if chosen carefully will bring pleasure throughout the year. Their initial cost may be high, but if this is spread over their period of life the total cost per annum is slight and they give good value. Unfortunately there is an impression, even among certain experienced gardeners, that all trees and shrubs will live forever and once they have been planted and have established themselves they can be forgotten, apart from an occasional pruning, some feeding, and some mulching. But this is not so. Many modern cultivars, or cultivated varieties, have only a limited life, sometimes as short as ten years or so. They lead a spectacular and rewarding life, but gradually their performance lessens and they either become drab and uninteresting or some of them may even give up the ghost and die, exhausted but fulfilled.

With most trees and shrubs a single feed once a year is usually sufficient to keep them in good health and maintain good performance. A mulch of moist peat, pulverized bark, farmyard manure, or garden compost should also be applied quite thickly around the base of the plant above the roots, particularly where the plants may be shallow rooting, as is the case with rhododendrons. So costs of maintenance here are not high, either financially or in terms of labour. If the plants are growing closely together they will tend to smother any weed growth below them, a tendency which can be further encouraged by heavy mulching or by the planting of ground covers, which means once again that general maintenance is not expensive.

### Fruit and Vegetables

Many gardens today are growing crops of fruit and vegetables for the first time, partly for economic reasons and partly because of a general heightening of interest in the environment and an appreciation of the nutritional and flavourful value of home-grown foods. Just how economical are home-grown fruits and vegetables? Does one really save money on them? Economy apart, it is certain that few foods are as enjoyable as those you have grown yourself.

The main answer to these questions is that it depends on the size of your plot. If it is small and very little space can be given to food crops, then those you do grow almost certainly cost more than you would have to pay for their equivalents in the shops, although they will be higher in nutritional value and better in flavour. But the phrase 'their equivalents in the shops' points the way to obtaining value here, for the answer is simply to grow those foods which are not generally available in the shops, or which are fantastically expensive.

For example, it would be absurd to grow a crop of King Edward potatoes on a small plot because the quantity obtained would not pay for the work involved, particularly when these same potatoes can be bought so easily in the local shops. But a crop of some variety unobtainable commercially, such as those served on the Continent, delicious, waxy, firm, and full of flavour, would be a very different thing; for here are potatoes not only for everyday eating but as a very special ingredient in a salad or with a tasty lamb chop. Certainly some of your guests will remember them with pleasure and your family ask you to grow them again.

If you find that strawberries take up space all the year round and produce their fruits only for a brief period, remember that they can be bought easily enough – you can even go and pick your own on some nurseries nowadays. Grow instead some of the alpines or perpetual fruiting kinds. You won't get huge crops at one time, but for many months of the year you will be able to collect a little handful almost every day, delicious in fruit salads, excellent in ice-cream and capable of being deep frozen for use during the lean months of winter. What is more, an edging of these little plants can be fitted into the shadier areas of the flower garden without looking out of place.

It is perfectly possible to grow a lettuce or two, some crisp radishes, a few flavoursome carrots, and prettily foliated beet in the flower borders if you have no space for a vegetable plot as such. Even if the area available to you is large, I suggest that these crops will still need to be grown, simply because they give such excellent value both monetarily and in flavour. These and other similar crops can be grown in succession so as to obtain constant supplies. This may make some demand on the space available, but this is probably less in the long run than the area demanded by long standing crops such as many of the brassicas, cabbages, cauliflowers, broccoli, and the like. The pleasing thing is that you need only sow small quantities of seed for successional crops; a pinch of lettuce seed, for example, as soon as the previous crop has germinated.

The size and needs of the family must be taken into account very carefully when planning which fruits and vegetables to grow, for with a large and growing family it is obviously desirable physically and financially to grow quantities of basic foods to keep them filled and healthy. When the children grow up and leave home the same large food crop is not required and can even be something of an embarrassment, unless arrangements can be made to dispose of surpluses to the local elderly or even contract for them to local shops. However, except for certain fruit trees which have a long life, most fruits and vegetables are grown very much on a year-to-year basis, and the emphasis on particular crops can be changed easily and quickly according to circumstances. If you have a little more leisure, you may find it enjoyable to grow something quite new to you, which once would have taken too much of your time; seakale or chicory, for instance.

So, with fruit and vegetables there really is very little that can be said against their cultivation so long as a sense of proportion is maintained about the individual foods to be grown and the quantities. Most vegetable seeds are so inexpensive that returns in the nature of several hundred per cent can be expected without great expenditure of energy. You will get most enjoyment if you relax and accept the fact that you are not growing for exhibition, but for your own satisfaction. Do not pay too much attention to the pundits.

It is possible to be carried away by vegetable gardening and become so imbued with a sense of purpose and virtue that one spends far more money than is necessary on equipment and on fertilizers, sprays, herbicides, fungicides, and insecticides. A powered cultivator is a waste on the vegetable patch unless it approaches half an acre or so in size, for it will probably lengthen the time taken for certain tasks such as digging, and the capital cost plus the cost of fuel will greatly outweigh the gains made on the crops. A few cloches will repay their modest price by the hurrying along of early crops and the extension of the season into the autumn. It is such a help to know that you can quickly rustle up a salad during winter, even if it is from leafy, not hearty, lettuce.

Cloches vary considerably in type and cost, but rather less in their effectiveness, for generally speaking all give a certain protection to young or tender crops, warming the soil, trapping the sun, and keeping out cold winds and even light frosts. Some have a comparatively short life, but as costs are low originally their price per working day turns out to be highly economical. This is largely because there is no running cost. Those who are gifted manually can often make their own cloches even more cheaply than they can be bought.

### The Greenhouse

A heated greenhouse is little more than a larger and artificially warmed cloche, but the difference in cost is surprising. The actual structure is comparatively cheap these days due to mass production methods, and most are well made and efficient, although as with most products the more one can afford to pay the better the article, as a general rule. It is the heating cost that counts, and although a cold greenhouse can be useful, it seems foolish to have this facility without making the most of it. The trouble is that the cost/temperature graph for heating a greenhouse appears to rise almost vertically!

For the average small greenhouse there are three fuels which can be used for heating, oil (paraffin), gas, and electricity. Paraffin heaters are much more convenient than they used to be, but they are still messy and can be smelly and damaging to the crop, in which case they are an annoyance and not a pleasure. They require constant attention if they are to perform efficiently. The heaters themselves are inexpensive, and the fuel they consume is again relatively cheap.

Gas heaters can be fed off the mains or from a supply of bottled or liquid gas. The former will obviously require expensive extensions of feed pipes from the nearest supply, probably the house, and if the greenhouse is situated some distance away this can be quite prohibitive. Nevertheless, considerable steps forward have been made with gas heating in the past few years, largely because of the expense of electricity, a form of power supply which seems to have all the advantages except price.

Once again electricity must be led into the greenhouse from the nearest mains supply and this can be an expense if some distances are involved. Proper copper-sheathed underground ducting is the safest, most foolproof long-term answer to the problem and this is inevitably expensive. Where comparatively short distances are involved it is sometimes possible to lead in an electricity supply by overhead wires, if necessary lifted above paths by stout poles. Get professional advice about your electricity supply. You may find that your local authority or your electricity board has laid down certain standards which you will have to observe.

The advantages of electricity outweigh the great disadvantage of running costs, however, for as a source of power it is extremely versatile. It provides light, it provides power for a number of different sources of heat, it provides ventilation and movement of air, and it can be adapted to provide an almost completely automated system. This means that the house can be left untended for complete days at a time, the necessary apparatus being switched on and off by clocks and thermostats, a great improvement on the old days.

But perhaps the most important virtue of electricity as a power source is that it is flexible enough to permit intelligent use. For example, it may cost £x per hour to warm the house by 1°C per 24 hours. Yet this 1°C will be used not so much for the benefit of all the plants in the house but to germinate certain seeds or to root certain cuttings. Then why heat several hundred cubic feet if only two or three are involved? Instead, for a comparatively modest outlay, it is possible to buy a small germination or propagation unit to place inside the larger house and this will consume only a fraction of the power needed to heat the entire house. If water is laid on as well as electricity, then a mist propagation unit can help even further, and cuttings from a single plant can quickly and easily be grown to populate the garden with very little cost and to grow enough little plants to pass on to friends.

Now all of this can consume time if one is interested and if one has this valuable commodity to spare. In fact, if you are looking for an interesting and useful way of passing time, this may be just the thing for you. On the other hand, if one is away at work, away on holiday, or even away out of the country, one great advantage is that it is possible to so programme an electrified greenhouse today that much creative work can be carried out without the necessity of being present the whole time.

Time really depends on how much you wish to spend, and so does money. The productive capacity of a greenhouse can be enormous if it is used intelligently, but it is only fair to say that if it is not used wisely, it can consist entirely of a drain on the pocket which produces little other than mistakes and frustrations. One should bear in mind that the house itself needs care and attention. It must be kept clean or pests and disease will take over; it must be looked after structurally or draughts and cold will enter; and it must be used intelligently and with understanding to obtain from it the undoubted advantages it can provide. However, there are many gardeners who will quite enjoy the routine involved.

A further advantage enjoyed by the greenhouse owner is that it provides shelter from the weather. Houses are available which are divided into two sections: potting and tool shed, and greenhouse. When the rains come down and one is eager to get on with a number of gardening tasks, then a greenhouse can be a real salve to the heart, for there is always much that can be done according to the season. But on the other hand one should face the fact that there are times when the weather will allow outdoor gardening although it is unpleasant and uninviting; and at this time it is all too easy to find a job in the greenhouse which has suddenly assumed a rather greater importance, perhaps, than it really deserves. A greenhouse can be an excuse to dodge discomfort and there are times when you may find it difficult to resist this excuse.

It is possible to grow a very few plants such as tomatoes directly in the soil of a greenhouse, and some people make a border holding all kinds of plants from orchids to tender shrubs if there is space; but as a rule all plants are grown in containers of some sort, mainly pots. They are thus immediately and conveniently portable. They can be brought into the home when they are at their decorative best, or in the reverse direction plants which have suffered from the dry air and lack of light after a long stay in the home can go back to the greenhouse for a period of convalescence and recovery. A greenhouse is of great benefit if you wish to overwinter some favourite plants, such as pot geraniums or pelargoniums, and other half hardy garden perennials, especially those grown in pots.

## Pots, Tubs and Containers

As a general rule this is the pleasure and benefit to be gained from all container-grown plants: they can be moved about from place to place according to need, weather, convenience, or whim. But there is more to it than that. Containers are versatile in that they can be filled with special soil mixtures to suit special plants; for example, acid, peaty mixtures for lime haters, and alkaline, chalky soils for lime lovers. They can be small, just flower-pot size, or they can be too large to move easily, in which case they can sometimes accommodate trees and shrubs of considerable size and maturity. There are certain fruits, figs for instance, which can stand outside in pots in summer and be given cover in winter.

Containers, tubs, pots, troughs, urns, or what you will, are essential to the decoration of a patio or terrace, for all paved areas, and for the creation of small, back-yard urban gardens, where often there simply is no space available for the usual features. They can vary widely in shape, size, and material, and of course in price. The most attractive containers are probably of stone or terracotta, two materials allied to the soil and hence psychologically and visually satisfying. But unfortunately many of these containers are now so expensive as to be quite prohibitive, although splendid work is being done by some manufacturers in the provision of good designs from reconstituted stone. Timber is not really a satisfactory material for a container, because however well it has been rot- and water-proofed, warping and decay is bound to take place after a while, and it is also a material which tends to harbour insect pests. Modern plastic tubs are a compromise which we must learn to accept and which are in many ways ideal, for they are light in weight, available in a wide range of shapes, designs, sizes, and colours, inexpensive, long-lasting, sterile, and easy to clean. Their texture may be unsympathetic to plants, but it will be found that if they are left outdoors for long periods they will produce a growth of algae on the sides which gives them a bucolic appearance. My own are becoming a pleasant Cotswold grey-green which matches the cottage walls, but it is likely that someone else would get more satisfaction from scrubbing them twice a year to give them back their original gleaming white.

There are, however, one or two distinct disadvantages to growing plants in containers. The main one is that they are expensive in time. While it is possible at most times of the year and in most locations to leave plants in beds and borders to themselves, trusting that they will obtain from mother earth the food and moisture that they require, all container-grown plants must be fed and watered frequently, watered as often as twice a day under certain circumstances. If you do this properly, results can often be beyond expectation, but it can be an intolerable burden for a person who is very busy or away from home each day. All containers, except the very largest or those with a special built-in reservoir of water, will dry out in a matter of hours on a hot and sunny or windy day, and the plants they contain will quickly die. One method of coping with this problem is to plunge the plants in flower-pots into larger containers filled with moist peat and to see that this is wetted at frequent intervals. It may also be possible to place containers in a shady place for the hottest hours of the day and bring them out when the sun has lost its main power. It is possible also to select plants which will tolerate such hot and dry conditions, for example pelargoniums and petunias, but not fuchsias. In certain circumstances it will be helpful, even essential, to install an automatic trickle irrigation system to keep the plant roots moist. This is not a difficult matter although it does involve a certain expense and unless carefully installed is apt to look ugly.

The initial cost of containers may be high, but if they are of sensible materials they will last for many, many years without needing replacement or repair.

All outdoor containers should have drainage holes in their bases, otherwise plants are apt to drown after summer showers, and the containers themselves apt to crack in winter frosts if they contain water. If you are in a position to choose containers from a source with a wide range available, look for one particular type which is not as readily available as it warrants. Containers of this type do not have drainage holes in the base but in the sides about an inch or two above the base, depending on size. This means that when the soil in them is watered a certain reservoir is always maintained at the base of the container, and this helps to feed moisture upwards by capillary action to the soil holding the roots. If this reservoir is kept filled with water it might become sour and smelly, so before filling the tub with soil, insert a layer of charcoal nuggets on the floor, reaching up to the level of the drainage holes. This will tend to absorb any smells.

I would not be without my collection of containers placed near the house. From the first show of crocuses to the last petunia, they bring continual pleasure. Most are used for the bulbs, which disappear when we plant them in the open ground, lilies, gladioli, and especially tulips. Some of these remain separate in pots, others like crocuses and tulips are planted deep down and have summer bedding plants above them.

## The Garden Pool

The making of a little garden pool is today not the major task that it was in the days when concrete was the only material from which a waterproof pool could successfully be made. But it is nevertheless a project which cannot or should not be completed in a matter of a day or two. The greatest effort is the physical digging out of the soil and placing it where required. The usual time- and labour-saving method is to dig out the pool area and pile the soil nearby so that a water splash can be built onto it and the mound can also be used for the creation of a rock garden. If these items are not required then the excavated soil will have to be thrown into barrows and wheeled away where it can be treated to make first-class potting soil or used in conjunction with the compost heap.

Modern pool-making depends on two types of material. The first, the simplest and the least expensive is an impervious sheet material, which is used merely to line the hole previously dug. This material can be simple plastic sheeting or it can be a thicker, tougher material, frequently a strong nylon fabric coated with a thick surface of plastic or artificial rubber. The thinner and less expensive materials tend to degrade in the sun and to last only a couple of years or so, a great pity when so much labour has gone into the digging of the hole. Heavier materials are said to have a life of many years, although my own experience revealed that although it lasted well and did not crack, split, tear, or rot, it was no match for the tiny teeth of ants belonging to a nest accidentally covered by the sheeting. However, another virtue of the material is that it is quickly and easily repaired, so no real harm was done.

Basically the process to follow is this. The hole is dug to the dimensions and depth required, in the chosen spot. The valuable top soil from the hole should be reserved for future use, separate from the sourer soil from the deeper part. It is not normally necessary to go deeper than about 3ft (1m) unless a very large pool is planned, for this depth will accommodate almost all types of decorative water plants. The shape of the excavation can be regularly round, square, or rectangular, or as irregular and curved as desired. If there is space, it is helpful to leave a shelf round the edge, 12-18ins deep, so that marginal plants can be placed on it. The walls of the excavation should slope slightly outwards from the base to the top.

When the hole has been dug to your satisfaction, it helps to line the base and if possible the sides with builder's sand mixed with a little peat so as to get a smooth surface with no projecting stones or pieces of root that may tear or puncture the skin of the sheeting. The size of the sheet required for a given hole is easily estimated. Whether the shape is regular or irregular, imagine it to be regular and order a sheet which is the length of the hole plus twice its depth and the width plus twice the depth. In other words, say you have an oval pool 10ft (just over 3m) long and 8ft (just under 3m) wide at the maximum points and 2ft (60cm) deep. Then the size of the sheet required will be 10ft + 4ft (just over 3m + 120cm) by 8ft + 4ft (just under 3m + 120cm).

This sheet should be laid over the hole and weights placed at several places around the perimeter so that it remains loosely stretched over the excavation. A water hose should then be brought in and if the jet is directed to the centre of the sheet the material will gradually stretch and sink downwards, the water pressure forcing it against the base and the sides. Water should be allowed to reach to within about 2ins (5cm) of the top. The weights on the material can then be removed, and to hide the somewhat ugly edge and to cover the excess material on the surface it is best to make an edging of paving stones or something similar which will overhang the water by just an inch or two. Small spaces can be left here and there between these stones to allow if necessary for a pipe to go into or come out of the pool, and the edging can also be planted with carpeting material such as thymes or rock phlox to soften the expanse of stone.

This is all there is to the basic construction of a small and simple garden pool. Water splashes, fountains, and the like can be somewhat more complex but still not out of reach for the ordinary gardener. Specialists and water-plant nurserymen offer catalogues dealing with all these items, and these include a great deal of information on all matters to do with garden pools, such as the items mentioned, in addition to fish and plants.

Another kind of garden pool, prefabricated and convenient but rather more expensive, is made from glass fibre and is available in a number of shapes and sizes. Because it is made to shape it is obviously impossible to make large pools by this means, but a wide variation in shapes is available. These preformed pools are rigid and inflexible, which means that when they arrive from the stockist it is necessary to dig a hole which fits them exactly so that they can be dropped into position. They never again require any attention, so far as is known.

Obviously the digging of a hole exactly to fit an irregular shape is a delicate proposition, and the only way to do it is by trial and error. Measure the dimensions and the shape as carefully as possible and drop the pool into the hole based on these at frequent intervals as it is being dug, gradually finding a close fit. It is better to have a hole slightly too large than one too small, for any gap between the soil and the fibreglass can be filled in again easily enough. Make sure all the time that bottom levels are maintained, for the water will always find its own level and will look quite extraordinary if higher at one end of the pool than the other.

Most of these preformed fibreglass pools have special deep portions built into them and shelving around the sides for marginal plants. They are also made with a slight lip which will rest on the soil surface around the perimeter. This is insufficient, however, to look natural or attractive, and the immediate area around the new pool should be paved or covered in such a way that there is a significant separation between the lawn and the pool. A paved surround also makes it easier to attend to the pool, to fill and empty it, to stock it, clean it, and to watch and feed the fish.

If you enjoy sitting by the water, as I do, make this area wide enough to take a stone seat or some chairs, so that even if it is only for a tea-break while you are weeding elsewhere, you can always enjoy the water at ease at a convenient moment.

A garden pool is a feature where the first cost, though considerable, can be almost the last. Pools should not need replacement or repair if they are installed correctly in the first place. Nor should they require much work, for a pool is a labour-saving feature in the garden so long as one takes the proper precautions and follows the proper methods. For example, once the new pool has been filled with water there should be an interval of at least a week for this to 'mature' before fish and plants are introduced. But in the meantime there is frequently dismay because the water, clear and limpid at the beginning, is seen to turn green and cloudy. Consequently it is drained away and fresh water is once again introduced. Exactly the same happens. But this is a natural course of events. The green, cloudy water is filled with microscopic life and this should be a welcome sign that it is alive and well. The introduction of fish and plant life will quickly bring it back to a clear state if the balance is correct. Once this is achieved you will discover that a pool is a complete little world of its own; just sit and watch it for a few minutes whenever you can.

Paradoxically, garden pools should be made where they will get the full sun and not under the shade of trees. Yet although the full sun should be on the surface of the water, the depths should be in the shade. The answer is to build the pool in the sun and to plant it with water lilies and other subjects which will effectively cover the water surface and so exclude the light from the depths. Ideally garden pools should grow water lilies (there are miniature forms for small pools), some marginal plants, and some submerged oxygenating plants, while some floating plants on the surface will help by cutting down the light to the interior of the pool. There should also be fish at a concentration of about 2-3ins (5-7cm) of fish to every sq. ft (0.093m²) of surface water, certainly no more. Give your plants a month or so to settle down and start growing before you put in the fish. Plants and fish together will ensure that the water clears after the first few weeks and that it remains clear.

One major problem with a garden pool is the way it appears to attract all the fallen leaves of the area once the autumn sets in. The answer to this problem is to cover the pool surface with netting at this time of year and clear the collected leaf fall regularly once a week so that no leaves, or only the smallest, can fall into the water. If many leaves are allowed into the water they will decompose and send off poisonous gases which will kill the fish. If you have made no provision to catch the leaves, skim them off the surface daily and place them in the compost bin.

Apart from leaves it is normally necessary to clean out a garden pool only once every three or four years. The best thing to do is to make a day of it. If you have young friends recruit their help, because fish, mud and water are involved. Empty the pool completely, placing the fish in a bucket or some other suitable receptacle. Plants can usually be left on the side if the work is not to take more than a few hours. The interior of the pool can then be cleared of any debris and any algae that may have accumulated on the sides can be gently scrubbed off. Take care that the lining is not pierced. Once this is done the water can be run in again and the fish returned to the pool. The plants may need a certain amount of attention in the form of the division of any which have become overgrown or the cutting away of roots which have grown outside the planting baskets.

In winter, if ice forms on the surface of the water it should not be broken by force, as this will set up shock waves in the water below which could stun or even kill some fish. If there is electricity available a small purpose-made heater will keep an area always clear; if not, then place a tin can on the ice and fill this with boiling water. When this has melted a hole in the ice, syphon or scoop out just a little water so that the ice stands clear of the water level. Try to keep this relatively small space clear of ice at all times. It is not the ice or the cold that affects the fish but the sealing of the surface so that gases given off by plant roots or any decaying leaves accumulate and poison the vital oxygen in the water.

## The Rock Garden

Earlier in these pages it was suggested that the soil dug out for the installation of a pool was frequently used for the creation of a rock garden. This is not essential, of course, but a convenience; and where it is put into practice it would be a pity and a waste to do it in a haphazard manner for a rock garden is not merely a mound of soil with some rocks on top. It is much more satisfactory if the digging of the pool and the construction of the rock garden are carried out as a joint operation. This facilitates the provision of the sharp drainage necessary to a rock garden and the installation of the rock. So the joint operation is likely to take considerably longer than the mere digging of the hole; but it will mean that the results are satisfactory both for their immediate appearance and their longer term success. If you are to enjoy it, plan it as an operation that will take some time, and once again recruit help if possible.

Stone for a rock garden can be ordered from many sources but it is wise to check exactly what one is getting. It is sometimes possible not only to order the exact type of stone one wishes to use, but actually to select the pieces. Try to use a stone which is more or less suited to the locality rather than one which is alien. Remember always that stone can be very heavy indeed and that if a load arrives at the front gate there must be some means available of transporting it down the garden to the site where it is wanted. One or two large and attractive pieces of stone are much more effective in appearance than several smaller pieces, and bear in mind also that, like an iceberg, most of the stone will lie beneath the surface, expensive as it may be. So choose the surface you wish to reveal and let this jut out from the slope in as natural a manner as possible. The top soil of the rock garden should be the top soil reserved from the pool if you are carrying out the two operations together. Mix in some sharp sand to help the drainage then fill in the soil by ramming under and between the stones, for a pocket of air can be disastrous for a plant's roots.

Equally a plant can drown if its roots lie in a natural pool of water trapped by a rock or by lack of efficient drainage. Before stacking up the soil to make the rock garden mound ensure good drainage by building on a base of rubble, old half bricks, broken stone, weathered cinders, concrete lumps, anything of that kind that is available. This should not be less than 6ins (15cm) deep and can be up to 2ft (60cm) or so depending on the size and height of the rock garden and the underlying soil. This will ensure that the soil in which the rock plants are to grow will at all times be as well drained as it would be on the side of a mountain.

The actual plants to be placed in position will be a matter of personal choice, but it is advised that they should be obtained from a specialist and that agreement should be sought on their suitability for the site. Many rock plants are delicate or particular in their requirements and require care in their planting and tending, and it would be a great pity if considerable expense and care went into a planting too short lived to give even a season's pleasure. Some plants cannot stand the damp of winter and few will put up with drips from trees above. There are a few tiny annuals which if grown *in situ* and carefully thinned out will prove delightful, but use them discreetly. Bear in mind when planting that your rock has been expensive, so do not hide too much of it under your plants.

A rock garden is a difficult place to weed, so try always to clear surfaces meticulously of all weeds when planting and to remove by hand all subsequent weeds as soon as they appear, while they are still small and capable of being plucked out without harm to surrounding rock plants. The scattering on the surface of rock chippings will help to serve as a kind of mulch to inhibit the growth of unwanted weed seedlings, although of course this should not be indulged to the extent that it disfigures the overall effect. Try to create a series of platforms from which you can work without either treading on plants or having to balance so precariously that work cannot be carried out effectively.

A rock garden is really what you make of it. Initial outlay can be heavy, both in cash and in labour, but subsequent costs will be low, although there will always be work to be done. As a garden feature a rock garden is not particularly dramatic unless it is on a large scale, but it can provide tremendous and constant interest.

If you decide that a rock garden is not for you, the soil you have excavated for the pool can be used in a number of other ways. It may be just what you need to level a certain spot, or it can be used to make a bank or mound to divide some section of the garden or provide protection. A herb bank is always an attractive and interesting feature, and by making the bank run from east to west you will provide a north and south side for herbs which respectively dislike or enjoy the sun.

## Paths, Drives and Patios

Still another pleasant garden feature that can cost much or little and cause much or little work is the framework of paths, driveways, courtyards, patios, or terraces that link one part of the garden with another. Most of these are paved in some manner because they are permanent features and because this makes them easier, safer, and cleaner to use. But this is not necessary and paths, for instance, can frequently be most attractive if of plain grass or perhaps random occasional paving-stones interplanted with low growing herbs such as thyme, which will give off pleasant odours when walked upon. If grass in one area is to be allowed to grow tall, one close-mown path will suffice and, if allowed to curve, will add much attraction to the scene.

There is, of course, a considerable difference between paths in the garden, leading, say, from the work area of toolshed and compost heap to the rose bed or vegetable patch, and the main driveway from road to garage, or the terrace outside the house. The garden paths are integral to the garden design and layout, and here plain concrete strips such as might be suitable for the entrance to the garage would look entirely out of place. Garden paths need to be sufficiently firm and dry underfoot not to disintegrate into mud and slush when used frequently in bad weather for foot traffic and for the wheeling of a heavy wheelbarrow or mower.

If the land covered is well drained, then I suggest that only the very occasional over-use or mistreatment can do serious damage to a grass walk or path, but if many journeys are to be made it can be helpful to install a stepping stone path, with paving stones set into the turf at pace intervals, just deeply enough to allow a mower to pass over them without harm and for the grass to hide the otherwise stark edges. There is no doubt that once a stepping stone path such as this has been installed it will cut down wear and tear on the grass and save possible annual treatment because of the compaction of the turf. The stones should be well laid, secure, and of sufficient weight not to move when a heavy barrow is pushed over them.

There is no need to hide or disguise the purely functional drive to the garage. If there is a dividing fence or wall running parallel to it, this can be used as a host for trained plants, both decorative and fruiting, and these will soften the approach considerably. This area might also be large enough for a narrow and slightly raised bed. But there should be no doubt what the drive is for and probably the best surface for it is concrete. This can be ribbed, brushed, or made to reveal the stone content according to preference, but it should be capable of doing its job, allowing the car easy and convenient access to and from the garage in all weathers. No trees or shrubs should be allowed to interfere with the vision here, but one or two creeping or ground cover plants can be allowed to advance over the edges of the concrete and so soften its hard lines. Never skimp on a drive or turning space. If too little room is allowed there will almost certainly be the constant irritation of scraped paintwork, bruised bark, shattered walls, or splintered wood. Remember that although you may be able to sail into your drive and up to the garage without any trouble, strange drivers or delivery men will not have such an intimate knowledge of the space available and may care little for any damage they may cause through their own carelessness.

If a turning place is necessary it does not follow that this should be of the same material as the main drive. It will be used far less frequently, either for its main purpose of turning the car to face the road or as occasional parking space when visitors arrive. It can well be of gravel, granite chippings, or if it suits the neighbourhood of one of the bituminous compounds. Again, allow plenty of space, for space means lack of worry, comfort, ease of management, and consideration for your visitors.

While plain concrete is suitable for the drive, it would be entirely wrong for the terrace or patio. These areas are both another room to the house and an extension of the garden into the home and as such they demand a much softer, more comfortable, more elegant treatment. They are best considered as living space, not working space. They should be paved, it is true, but with a more sophisticated material than concrete, and there is a wide choice of materials available. There should be sufficient space for chairs and a table, as well as for plants in containers to decorate the area. There can be trellises on the walls and a pergola overhead, both of which can carry plants to soften the atmosphere and serve again as a link between house and garden. The paving should have the slightest of slopes away from the house to carry heavy rainwater safely away and a low wall around the perimeter will emphasize the fact that this is an extra room to the house that happens, incidentally, to be projecting into the garden. You might enjoy making this a double wall, in effect a long trough-like container, so that it can be filled with soil and plants.

Although the making of a terrace can be initially expensive, one basic cost that should not be skimped is that of preparation, groundwork, the creation of the foundations. Concrete merely poured on to the soil surface will crack and crumble. Paving stones set on the ground will rock and sink and provide an uneven and unsafe surface. Do bear in mind that this area will be used frequently.

The site should be excavated to a depth of at least 6ins (15cm) and 3-4ins (7-10cm) of hardcore should be well rammed into place to provide a sound foundation. Concrete can be poured directly on to this and where paving slabs for a patio are laid in concrete the ultimate in security and long life will be obtained. But this is not vital. A thick layer of sand on top of the compacted foundation will make a perfectly adequate bed for paving stones under most circumstances, a considerably quicker and less expensive method.

Better spend the money thus saved on some good outdoor furniture, for the patio is a place to be enjoyed and if convenient and pleasant it can be used for summer morning breakfasts as well as summer afternoon siestas and evening entertaining. Remembering that it is a part of the garden, use plenty of plants. Never allow it to be a store place for garden tools, a dumping place for bales of peat or even a clear place in which to saw some wood for winter burning. Its function is for leisure living and enjoyment, and if you keep it that way it will bring you much pleasure.

The conscientious laying of paving is expensive in cash, labour, time, and effort, but if it is properly done it should never need touching again, which means that its first cost is also its last. If it is badly done it will be a constant irritation and a constant cost. When paying out for materials and possibly for labour it may be difficult to be philosophical, but if possible try to average out your total costs over a period of, say, twenty years, in which case they appear far more reasonable. Better still, think of the considerably increased value of your home as a result of your labours and your layout of cash.

Throughout this chapter I have tried to look at a number of basic garden features and evaluate them in terms of cost in time, energy, labour, and finance. In many cases, such as this last, the initial cost should also be the final one. Sometimes, as with vegetable gardening, costs may be low but they recur year after year, although the produce gained will almost certainly show an overall profit.

In every case you, the gardener, can make up your own mind how to tackle your problem. Your decisions will not always be your own but may be dictated by the needs of a growing family, by lack of cash, by advancing age, or by any one or more of a number of outside influences. What I try to do in the succeeding pages is to suggest ways in which the best results can be obtained by the easiest and most pleasant means. If gardening is a chore it will not be carried out well. If it is a pleasure, then the results are sure to be effective.

But not all of us know that this or that recommended procedure is unnecessary. 'I always tell people to double dig their gardens but I never do it myself,' one of England's famous gardeners told me only a few days ago. So don't be afraid to break the rules; I often do, and with success. Much of standard gardening practice has been handed down through the years from one head gardener to another and so into the pages of the gardening magazines and books. What we fail to understand is that some of the operations said to be vital were originally devised largely to keep the under gardeners or the apprentices busy and out of mischief. When the master or mistress strolled through the gardens it was essential that all of the garden staff should appear to be engaged in urgent and probably violent activity, and so jobs were created, partly in order to retain a large staff and partly to keep young Jim in a job, him with the widowed mother.

Now that we do our own gardening we can do away with un-necessary jobs and concentrate on those that are vital. This will give us much more time, so much more energy, and perhaps even so much more money that we can enjoy our leisure in the garden as well as our activities.

# 3

## GRIN AND WEAR IT

We are all individuals, with personal appearance, personal finger-prints, and a personal disposition made up partly by genetic chance, partly by environmental influence, and partly by force of circumstance. Because of the many different influences that have made us what we are we tend to consider ourselves quite unique and we do not believe that any other person can have quite the same interests, attitudes, problems, or outlooks. Many other people do, in fact, have the same interests, attitudes, problems and outlooks, but the fact that they have them in different degrees or that they have them in conjunction with many other individual attributes produces in the end a series of different pictures rather than one identikit.

In exactly the same way every garden is an individual with characteristics all of its own. No other garden is exactly the same. Other gardens may have the same soil analysis, the same water table, the same climate, and the same plants, but this one will be differentiated by reason of its shape, the pruning of its roses or the number of its goldfish. Every physical aspect of a garden helps to create its special character, even the personality, the energy, the eyesight, or the wealth of the gardener.

Most of the elements which have an effect on the character of a garden are basic. Some can be changed with effort, time, and determination, but others will always exist and nothing the gardener can do will make any real and permanent difference to it. He will have to grin and wear it.

If I may be allowed to interject a personal note, our own garden is today completely unlike the garden we took into our care many years ago. It is totally different in character, in appearance, and in productivity. But certain basic elements remain exactly the same and we will never be able to change them. The garden is long and narrow, running east to west. It is on a hillside and situated in a funnel so that all the winds from the Atlantic Ocean condense, conform, and compress themselves into an aerial demon which hurls itself shrieking and shattering onto and into our plot, determined to inflict as much pain and do as much damage as can be imagined. The plot is a levelled portion of the hillside, which means that although water gurgles all around us there is none but our tiny pool on our land. The few old trees that still exist are ancient rather than elderly. The soil is limy and the entire area is surrounded by farmland. Local wildlife is more at home on our land than we are ourselves.

We have done over the years what we can to alleviate some of the pains and perils due to these physical characteristics and to some extent we have succeeded, but we will never be able to alter the orientation, the climate, the lie of the land, the wind patterns, the depth of the soil, and the age old pathways of the wildlife. We cannot change the shape of the property but we can alter the content. We cannot change the direction of the prevailing wind but we can build windbreaks to give some protection to certain plants. We cannot alter the basic pathways of the wildlife, but we can protect some of our fruit and vegetables by surrounding them with netting. So long as they are not performing a wind resistant role we can take out hedges to allow more space, more access of the soil to light and air, and we can dig out the roots of ancient trees so that they may be replaced with younger, stronger, more prolific types. We cannot alter the shape of the garden, but we can alter its appearance and disguise its shape by making of the long, narrow strip a series of different and individual gardens.

These imposed conditions, these things we find on and in our plots when we first take them over, are of considerable importance, for they dictate to us to some degree the way we will garden in the future. Some are problems, others are bonuses. Whatever they are they force us into certain channels by the mere fact that they are there. For instance, a fine old walnut tree growing in a corner of the garden as it has done for the past 200 years will not be cut down and destroyed unless it becomes dangerous, for apart from the intrinsic value of the tree as a garden feature, the sheer difficulty of the task makes one shy away from it. The 8ft wall built along the northern boundary of the garden so that it faces due south is too precious an example of free solar heating for it to be ignored or neglected, and with its protection trees, climbers, and herbaceous plants can be grown where it would otherwise be impossible.

Perhaps the most important imposed condition is that of the soil in our gardens. It can be acid or alkaline, clayey or sandy, light or heavy, shallow or deep, boggy or well drained, rich or poor. When we discover these things we are faced with a choice: either we spend the remainder of our gardening life fighting the condition of our soil or we accept the limitations imposed and adapt our mode of gardening and the plants we grow to the pattern laid down for us.

This is, perhaps, the greatest lesson of all in easy gardening. You can make your gardening so much more a pleasure if you co-operate with nature rather than fight it.

We garden on the oolitic limestone of the Cotswolds, which means of course that our soil is alkaline and unsuited to the growing of such calcifuges as rhododendrons, azaleas, and some heathers. We could grow them for brief periods, after which they would gradually sicken and then die. We could grow them with considerable difficulty if we dug out holes in the soil, lined these with heavy polythene sheeting and filled them with an acid soil mixture. This would mean that neither the natural limestone soil would touch the plant roots, nor would alkaline water coursing through the soil after rain. But again this would mean only a temporary way of growing calcifuges.

Because we liked them and because they would give us varied colour at a time when there was little but yellow, we were determined to grow a small and limited number of calcifuges and realized that the only way we could succeed on a long term basis would be to provide a completely alien soil for them. So gradually over the years we built up what became known as our peat mound. As the name suggests, it is composed mainly of peat plus considerable quantities of home-made compost and grass mowings, the latter held in place by walls made of peat bricks. The whole exercise was, frankly, uneconomic in time, labour, and money, for it was expensive in each of these. But it was an experiment and a challenge and it eventually brought pleasure for some years. When it had eventually reached some 30ft by 10ft by 3ft high, we began planting our rhododendrons and azaleas, with some heathers at their feet. For years they flourished, supported by the constant addition of further peat mulches through the years and annual heavy waterings with sequestrene, a chelated iron product which in effect increases the acidity of the soil.

And then in a single summer we lost the lot. It was the exceptional drought of 1976, and although we collect and store something like

1000 gallons of rain water, this soon went. Our only other source of water was from our well, heavily alkaline and in desperately short supply. So the peat mound went unwatered and the shallow rooting rhododendrons, azaleas, and heathers wilted, browned, and died.

It was an experiment and in some ways it was successful. We regret the loss of these plants but we are glad we had them for the time we did. Nevertheless, I will be the first to admit that to grow plants in this manner is not a practical proposition for the average gardener. It may be better for him to curb his desire for plants alien to his district and grow instead the many plants that will flourish in his own soil.

Although it is not generally possible to change the nature of a soil, except perhaps under concentrated attack over a number of years, all soils can be improved, which is to say made more conducive to the successful growing of plants. Digging lets air and light into the soil and the application of such materials as farmyard manure, compost, peat, spent hops, straw, grass clippings, and the like will all help to give a richer soil of a more open texture, for in decaying they accelerate bacterial activity in the soil, which in turn unlocks plant foods in solution to the thirsty roots. Bear in mind, though, that in time heavy applications of humus tends to make the soil slightly more acid than it was originally.

So by all means try to improve your soil, but do not attempt to change it except in small patches. Far better if you wish to grow rhododendrons in an area of calcareous soil to plant them in tubs or other large containers where you can feed them with special acid soil mixtures. Rhododendrons, azaleas, camellias, all acid soil lovers, make splendid container plants.

Take advantage of every aid offered to you by nature. For example, if your soil is a heavy clay, exhausting and frustrating to work and to break down to a fine tilth, then call on nature in the form of winter rains, snows, and frosts. Dig the soil as roughly as you like, leaving great lumpy clods lying on the surface. By the early spring the rains and frosts will have broken this down into a fine crumbling texture far better than you could produce yourself. Help it further by adding to it bonfire ash, home-made compost, and lawn mowing mulches.

Another physical aspect of our gardens that is presented to us in the beginning and will be there after we have gone is the aspect or orientation, the north, south, east, and west of the garden. This can be a matter of the greatest importance, and yet there is nothing we can do to change it. Or is there?

The aspect of a garden becomes an irritation or a drawback when it provides either more shade than we wish or it provides this shade in the wrong place. If the shade is interjected by the house or a neighbouring building, then it is obviously impossible to remove or alter this obstruction. Once again it is a question of co-operating with circumstances rather than fighting them. If the shade is from some large object such as the house, then it will itself be of significant size and where it lasts longest it might be advisable to grow some of the shade tolerant plants. But all shade moves, and what may be dark in the morning can be light in the afternoon, and this is where a certain intelligent observation and planning can be of help.

Let us take once again the example that the house places a part of the garden in shade in the morning and leaves it to the sun in the afternoon. Obviously it will be to our advantage to make the most of this period of light, so we should be careful not to plant a tall and spreading tree where it will merely perpetuate the dark shade of the morning. Again, there are certain plants for which it is considerable help to have morning shade and afternoon sun, particularly those of a tender nature such as peaches and camellias. If winter frost on these plants is too suddenly warmed off by early morning sun, great damage can be done. The buds need to thaw out gradually in the shade, so that by the time the sun travels around the corner and touches the branches they are ready and receptive.

There can be cases where the sun moves around the corner of the house but instead of bathing the garden in its warmth another building, or a high wall, or a tree then intervenes and so the garden is in perpetual shade. There is little that can be done in these circumstances except to grow shade tolerant plants, of which there are a fair number, including all the spring flowering bulbs. On the other hand, never give in without a fight. Is it possible to have that wall lowered by just a couple of bricks? Is it possible to have that tree trimmed to allow in just a little more light? Is it possible to alter that line of shrubs or move that tree a little to the right? Is it possible to replace that solid brick wall with one of pierced screen walling? Is it possible, even as a last resort, to paint that wall white so as to bring reflected light at least into the darkness?

Only in exceptional circumstances is it possible to do anything about the size of our gardens. Only rarely is it possible to buy a piece of land adjoining and seldom is it possible or desirable to sell off a piece of the garden to someone else. But just as one can alter the appearance of the shape, so it is possible under certain circumstances to alter the *appearance* of the size of the garden.

No garden other than the smallest of the urban backyard types should ever be visible at a single glance from a single viewpoint. There should always be an element of mystery or the unknown, so that what lies around the corner should be a perpetual question. The dividing walls need not be high nor obtrusive; a single shrub can hide the unexpected pool or the herb garden. Two cordon apples can make a screen, even a row of attractive climbing beans, or a trellis of climbing squash through which it is easy enough to see, can somehow completely conceal the vegetable garden on the other side.

One of the best ways to enlarge a small garden is to take greater advantage of the dimension of which there is plenty, the vertical. Cover the walls of the house and any other walls or fences with climbing or clinging plants and you extend not only the total area of growing green but the actual horizon, for the wall instantly looks further away.

But choose your walls with care, for they can be a valuable help to the gardener. Never waste a hardy ivy plant, for example, on a wall which basks in the sun for most of the day. Give the ivy a north or east wall to cling to and it will be perfectly happy. Save the south-facing wall for something more precious and exotic, something you might never be able to grow outdoors without its assistance, a passion flower, a vine, a peach, or some unusual flowering climber for instance. Remember, too, with all walls and screens that to be effective they need not be thick and heavy. All walls, hedges, or fences around the perimeter of a property exist to determine and indicate legal boundaries and some of them, or parts of some of them, are helpful or pleasant in that they provide a modicum of personal privacy, so that the neighbours or passers-by cannot easily see to criticize your sloth if sunbathing or your technique if pruning your roses. Some walls and other screens are helpful as wind-breaks, yet once again a light obstruction here is actually more efficient than a heavy one.

So if you have plenty of space and can therefore freely choose your various locations for plants of different types, then by all means erect huge, high and thick walls in places, for they can make dramatic and effective backdrops for a bush of blossom or even have a tapestry of differing colour and texture woven through them to give rich and subtle effects. But if your space is limited, try to keep all screens light and airy, thus saving space and providing more light to the interior, while at the same time providing a sufficiency of shelter from prying eyes and from the more intemperate excesses of the wind.

Yet one can take these various steps to provide a light and airy interior and still have it shaded at important parts of the day by the overbearing and overpowering branching of one or more large trees. The task of removing one of these is almost prohibitive without the expense of skilled labour, for in small spaces a large tree has to be taken down piece by piece. Again, to take a tree down to ground level is a comparatively simple matter today with the assistance of power saws, but to dig out and remove the huge roots left behind is a major problem that can involve the destruction or despoliation of much of the total area of the garden. It will also be found in some areas that tall and significant trees are protected by preservation orders and that you will not be permitted to take them down unless you can prove them dangerous, so check with your local authority first.

Fortunately large trees have spreading branches which carry vast numbers of leaves which feed and sustain the tree. This means that we can remove a few branches here or there and trim back others without endangering the life of the tree in any way. Any branches which are low enough to impede progress through the garden should be removed close to the main trunk, the exception of course being those trees which are of a naturally weeping habit of growth. By removing some of the lower branches not only is working and walking in the garden made easier and safer, but much more light is allowed under the tree, encouraging the growth of plants hitherto found impossible in that location. As the years have passed in our own garden we have found that this has become almost an annual operation. Remove particularly branches whose tips come down dangerously to eye level.

It is helpful with old and large trees to have them examined and serviced every ten years or so, perhaps more frequently, particularly when one grows fairly near the house. This is an expense which may not be strictly necessary and should be indulged in only if it can be afforded financially and if the wellbeing of the tree is a matter of some concern. However, we have gained much pleasure in knowing that we have been able to prolong the lives of our ancient walnut and Pitmaston Duchess pear this way. After a really brutal gale we get in touch with a tree surgeon friend who does in hours what would take us days or what would even be impossible for us to attempt at all.

Make sure that a competent, qualified, and insured tree specialist is engaged to carry out the task, for there are many unqualified gangs who can do more harm than good and charge wildly unrealistic prices. Go to a firm which is a member of a recognized professional body and insist on an inspection and a written estimate before allowing work to go ahead. What a tree surgeon of this type will do to what is apparently a healthy though old tree is look for cavities in the main structure in which rain water and fallen leaves can collect, branches which are dead or rubbing against others, and any evidence of splitting or strain. Cavities will be cleaned out like the cavities in a tooth and then treated and stopped with some sterile material, perhaps concrete. Where it is too large or deep the cavity may be tapped, a hole being driven through at the lowest point so that any rain gathering will automatically drain out again. Weak, dead, dying, or rubbing branches will be removed and all wounds treated and sealed. Where major branches have grown large and heavy so that there is danger of them splitting or snapping, a good treeman will support one branch by another by means of steel guy ropes.

These treatments, admittedly a luxury, can add fifty years to the life of a fine old tree. They can also ensure that there is no danger that a weakened branch might fall and damage either people or property.

Another problem that faces some gardeners when they take over a new plot is to find that their land slopes so significantly that they have difficulty in tending it, let alone producing a garden which is both attractive and productive. When we look at this problem our doctrine of co-operating with the plot and its basic conditions rather than fighting it appears to lose its validity. If we accept the slope we may find that we can grow nothing on it except some ground hugging and soil anchoring plants such as grass or the rose of sharon, *Hypericum calicynum*, and if we are content with this then we will certainly have a garden which is easy to tend.

Most of us will insist that we should have some level area on which we can grow normal crops, and this will involve terracing the garden, a considerable task that involves the moving of large quantities of soil and the installation of strong soil-retentive walls, a major undertaking indeed.

I suggest that under circumstances such as these every effort should be made to seek a compromise, one that does not necessitate the complete terracing of large areas nor mean the growing of dull ground cover plants merely as a means of holding the soil in position. It is possible by the careful planting of certain shrubs to anchor the soil of a slope so that an area can be cleared and the slope lessened for some feet. On a very moderate slope it will even be possible to grow most vegetables and some fruit such as strawberries, the lines running across the garden rather than up and down the slope. A further belt of shrubs, low-growing and root-spreading, below this cleared portion will again anchor the soil and protect yet another area for more normal gardening. There is no reason why an attractive interesting, and productive garden should not be created by compromises such as these.

# 4

## HOW TO EASE TASKS IN SPECIFIC AREAS

### Lawns

A lawn is basic to a British garden, due partly to tradition and partly to the fact that our climate is particularly favourable to the growing of fine grasses. Certainly no other material makes a better setting for the more colourful plants of all kinds that are normally set around and sometimes in a lawn. A lawn is usually the first garden feature that is begun when a new garden is made, both because it provides basic furnishing for the plot in the least possible time and because it provides within weeks a surface which can be walked on and played on. It is like a carpeted room. Once the floor is covered we can furnish in our own time. Lawn can easily be cut into to make beds or borders, it can be dug to make a vegetable patch, it can have holes made for the planting of trees and shrubs, it can be excavated for the creation of a water garden and it can be built upon by a garden shed, garage, and even rock garden. So obviously it is a useful as well as an attractive feature.

A lawn consists of a very large number of individual grass plants growing closely together. Surprisingly, perhaps, the roots of some of these plants can go down as much as 5ft ($1\frac{1}{2}$m) into the ground, and therefore deep and thorough cultivation of the soil is advisable when making a fine lawn. If there is likely to be a drainage problem, then this should be attended to before the lengthy process of making the lawn has begun and land drains should be inserted where this appears necessary. There should also be a layer of drainage material such as coarse sand, shingle, or even pebbles so that at no time does the fine surface of the lawn become over-wet. Ideally pipes should also be laid under the soil to provide for an automatic watering system, because an efficiently drained soil will have a tendency to dry out quickly.

It all sounds highly complex, even daunting, and of course it is;

and if gardening is to be a pleasure for us the making of an elaborate lawn of this nature is not for us. There are easier, quicker, and cheaper ways of obtaining a lawn perhaps not quite so perfect, but quite adequate for almost all normal purposes, and subsequent care and attention can greatly improve an existing lawn without resort to extreme measures.

It is probably true that most gardeners have inherited their lawns, in which case they have been presented with a moderately level or perhaps evenly sloping sward, liberally dotted with weeds and coarse grasses and with occasional bumps and hollows. There is a temptation to dig it all in and start from the beginning again, but unless you really want to labour this is unnecessary and it will create a great deal more work than is needed to improve the lawn significantly.

The key to the transformation of a coarse grass surface to a good lawn is regular mowing. This regular mowing will get rid of many weeds because of the sheer persistence with which they are cut down, during which process the crowns of the toughest kinds become damaged. This regular mowing will also reveal any uneven portions, and it is worth while dealing with these immediately, even in mid-run with the mower.

If the uneven portion is a bump or a hollow, both are dealt with in the same way so long as they are of manageable proportions, say no more than a yard or so square. The process here is not to skim off some of the grass from the top of the bump or add some soil where there is a hollow, but to cut an H into the surface about 3 or 4ins deep (8-10cms) and roll back the two tongues of turf which have been made. Scrape out a little of the underlying soil in the case of a bump and add some good soil or compost in the case of a hollow. Then replace the two tongues of turf, tread them firmly into place and carry on with your mowing. Next time you cut the grass you will see whether your administrations have done the trick and can repeat the process or adjust it if necessary.

A lawn is only as good as its edges. No matter how perfect the surface, how smooth and green, if it is surrounded by a shaggy and unkempt boundary then it is downgraded at once. Edge trimming is as necessary as mowing, and the process of neatening these edges has an important secondary bonus. It has surprised me to find that some people find this operation a bore. For my part it is the only time I see every inch of a border closely and I enjoy this. As you go around the perimeter of the lawn clipping the edges, bending low with hedge shears, standing more comfortably with long-handled edging shears, or even trundling along with a battery powered edge trimmer, you cannot fail to notice that certain plants are doing well, that some are seeding themselves, and you may also see faults in the beds and borders as you pass them, faults which you can often right immediately. Perhaps you see an unexpected and hitherto unnoticed outcrop of weeds, perhaps an infestation of aphids, perhaps a broken stem. You notice gaps and consider what plant might do well there. You may even have one, a chance seedling, in some other place, which you can go and water right away and move when your edge clipping is finished. These are things you could so easily miss except for the comparatively slow and even progress you make while trimming the edges. Perhaps I should say here that my personal choice for a trimmer is a pair of long-handled shears.

Weeds in the lawn are easily dealt with today. Probably the best way of handling them is to go over the whole area of the lawn carefully with a mechanical spreader holding a special feed-and-weed lawn mixture which both encourages the fine grasses to grow and to green effectively while it simultaneously kills the broad leaved weeds. I advise that this should be done carefully, because if there is overlapping the doubled application can be so strong as to show itself in long strips of burnt turf; and if there is a gap between rows with the applicator this will show up as strips of shorter and lighter-toned grass. One application a year is really necessary, two are better, and three are generally unnecessary. It is true that this treatment will encourage the strong growth of grass and hence increase the necessity for mowing, but a moment's thought will show that one cannot cut the grass once a week or more often for most of the months in the year without weakening the plants. They obviously need feeding.

However effective the lawn sand in the mixture may be in killing existing broad-leaved weeds, some will survive, or possibly will germinate and grow after the granules have been applied. So for the early part of summer it is helpful to watch for these weeds while mowing and to treat them individually with a hormone or selective weedkiller. The application of this is a matter of moments, but it is a stitch in time process, for weeds can multiply at a surprising rate if they are left alone. I once had a neighbour who never walked down the garden without an old kitchen knife, his weed knife. At every journey he bent and dug out any weed which caught his eye. It was the only weedkiller he used and he had a beautiful lawn!

It is a relatively simple matter to take over a coarse and neglected lawn and make something finer of it, but what about starting from scratch? What if you are faced with an uneven, lumpy, littered expanse, with occasional puddles, odd pieces of timber, broken bricks, and lumps of concrete, with waist-high nettles in one corner and a tangle of brambles in another?

There is a great temptation under these circumstances to look at the worst side, say that you must start from the beginning and dig and clear the entire garden. So you start at one end and begin to dig, clearing the weeds and the rubble as you go. It will take a long time and a great deal of energy, and by the time you have completed the task the weeds will be growing again where you first began. You need not do it this way.

You may prefer to take a chance and compromise. First clear the rubble and put it carefully to one side. Some of it may come in useful as foundation material for the drive to the garage or for the patio paving. When you can walk about safely without tripping over a baulk of timber or a lump of concrete, spray your weeds with one of the weedkillers that does not persist in the soil. You will probably need to repeat the process after a time, but never mind, all weeds are cowards and if attacked strongly and constantly they always give in.

Now begin your levelling process. Don't be too thorough to begin with, just skim off the hills and deposit the extra soil in the hollows. A little light forking and raking will be involved here and gradually you will find that the ground begins to level out. Even the slight amount of cultivation involved will improve the condition of the soil.

Ideally the thing to do now is to buy in a few loads of good top soil and spread this over the surface of the garden. But this will be so expensive in time, labour, and money that one must normally forget ideals and return to the practicalities of compromise. Instead, invest in a few bags of peat and spread this over the surface of the soil. Even a very thin layer so that the soil beneath shows through will still be of real and significant benefit. Rake the surface as level as you can get it without going to great trouble with pegs and spirit levels but judging by careful observation, and then sow your grass seed or lay your turf.

There are several types of grass seed and the type you should choose will depend on how much you wish to spend and the use to which the lawn will be put when it is completed. I suggest that for the average lawn of the average house the finest grades are a waste of money, for they are considerably more expensive than the coarser grades. On the other hand the very coarse grasses, composed largely of rye grass, are really more suitable for a paddock than a lawn. They will grow more quickly, requiring more frequent mowing and they will tend to allow the growth of weeds between the individual tufts of grass. Go for a medium mixture with a small proportion of rye grass and this will give a reasonably fine turf with the strength and vitality to stand up to the thunder of tiny feet or even the trundling of a wheelbarrow over its surface.

It is possible to sow the seed using the feed and weed granule applicator that has been mentioned earlier so long as it has been carefully washed out. Or you will find that you can probably hire a seed spreader from a garden centre or a tool hire specialist. It will generally be worth the money unless only a very small area is to be sown, and it will certainly result in a more even spread of seed than you can manage by hand. But if you do apply your seed by hand, then do it in two separate applications, one up and down the garden and one across. This will mean dividing your seed into two equal portions (preferably putting just a little aside to use in case you find one or two gaps later on) and allowing a total for the two applications of about 2oz (50g) per sq yd (m²).

Rake in the seed very lightly when you have finished or sprinkle over it a very light layer of granulated peat. The soil should preferably be moist but not wet, and if it is dry it will be worth your while to sprinkle the entire area with water at a rate of at least a gallon per sq. yd. (5 l. per m²), doing this very gently and evenly so as not to wash the new seed out of the ground.

If birds, particularly sparrows, are a pest in your garden it may be worth your while to protect your newly sown seed. Practically all grass seed today comes ready dressed with a bird repellent powder, but although this sometimes works, other birds are probably unable to read for they pay no attention at all. The trouble is not so much that the birds eat the seeds but that they pull up the tiny germinating seedlings or they make dust baths in the fine soil. You can keep the birds off the newly sown patch by sticking a series of twigs in the ground and winding black cotton between these so that you protect the whole surface. This isn't an easy thing to do and my own findings suggest that birds always *seem* to do more damage than they in fact do.

Depending on the weather, the grass will begin to germinate in ten days or so, and in twenty days you should see a fine fuzz of grass over the entire lawn. You will also see a number of new germinated weeds, but try to ignore these for the time being. Do not walk on the grass and do not attempt to cut it until it is about 2in (5cm) high. If the area is small enough, or if your patience is strong enough, try to cut the grass then with a pair of sharp shears rather than with a mower. The exception might be if you have a very light electric mower with newly sharpened blades. The trouble is that the grass roots are young and have not yet got a good hold on the soil. There is a strong possibility that blunt cutters will pull many of the tiny plants out of the soil or will so loosen the roots in the soil that the plants fail to develop satisfactorily. Subsequent cuttings can be more or less normal, but for the first few months never cut the grass too low. The weeds that appeared at the same time as the grass can be plucked out by hand, gently so as not to move adjoining grass plants. Or you can use a special type of hormone weedkiller called Weedkiller for New Lawns. Ordinary weedkillers will tend to burn the young grasses and can do real damage, and if you try to use them in a dilute form you will merely find that they fail to act at all.

Laying turf instead of sowing grass seed provides a much quicker result and this is its only virtue as a method. It is very much more expensive and a good turf today is difficult to find. Too much so-called turf is mere meadow grass, complete with all the weeds one sees in a farm meadow. There are sources of super turf, some of it grown under scientific conditions, sometimes by some type of hydroculture, but prices are normally prohibitive here, the product being used normally for trade stands at agricultural and horticultural shows.

However, if you do have a source of good turf and wish to use it in order to get a quickly usable lawn, all the preparatory stages are identical. The turf will probably arrive in rolls, each separate piece being about 3ft (1m) long and 1ft (30cm) wide, although they are sometimes 12in (30cm) square. Stand on a board as you lay the turves so that you do not compact the soil too much. Lay the turves as you would lay bricks, with joints overlapping rather than level. Make sure that each turf is the same thickness as the previous one. Keep gaps to a minimum and where they show scatter a little good soil over them. Beat the grass lightly with the back of a spade to establish a good close contact between the soil and the turf, then tread the whole area once the job has been completed, so that the grass is well compacted and so that you can discover any gaps, humps, or hollows. Deal with these at once. Water thoroughly and in two or three weeks it will be evident that roots have grown down into the soil and new growth is appearing on the surface. Again make the first cut or two very delicately, for those roots are only adhering lightly to the soil below. Never allow the turves to get dry and when you water make sure that the whole of the turf and the soil below has been adequately moistened.

Once the grass has become established, whether sown or grown from turves, it will require to be cut regularly during the warmer months. It is the regularity of cutting that produces a good sward. This process of mowing the lawn must therefore be repeated at intervals of at least once a week from as early as March or April through to October or November, always depending of course on the weather; do not attempt the task when the grass is wet or frosted. This mowing can be a real chore, and in order that this shall not be the case it is possible to seek out the irritations and deal with them, so that mowing the lawn becomes no more than taking a walk in the garden.

So long as your mower is efficient and suited to its task and your capabilities, the irritations of lawn mowing come with the necessity of emptying the grass box at frequent intervals and the stopping and starting necessitated by difficult corners, narrow spaces, hills and dips, banks, paving which is proud of the lawn surface, over-hanging plants (so that you either behead the flowers of the border or leave a strip of taller grass below), low branches so that you have to duck your head or get slashed across the face, sticks or stones on the surface, or perhaps a dog's bone or a child's toy.

A quick walk around the garden before mowing begins will enable you to see some of these potential causes of trouble and remove them. A few bamboo canes pushed carefully and diagonally against a plant will hold it back away from the edge and the cane is easily removed later. Some of the other problems are the result of poor design, and instead of putting up with them it will be helpful to energy and temper if they are corrected as quickly as possible, usually a comparatively simple matter involving the creation of a curve instead of a right angle or the widening of a pathway to allow free passage of the machine. The problem of the emptying of a grass box can be eased by the dotting about on the lawn of two or more large pieces of plastic sheeting, hessian, old sheets, or some such material at convenient locations, so that each time you pass you can stop, empty out the grass, and then continue again. The mound of grass will grow and can be towed away easily enough to be used as a mulch or for composting.

To avoid one problem, instead of planting a tree or shrub in a round or square hole, make this shaped like a leaf or an oriental eye, and the mower can then glide easily past the obstruction without having to stop to make special movements.

Where the grass is of a coarse nature and has not been allowed to grow too long, it is possible to leave it lying on the ground rather than collect it in the grass box of the mower. This will save considerable time and trouble, but it is not to be recommended as a general practice, because the grass lying on the surface tends to choke that which grows below. In the time of drought it is nevertheless a helpful method of providing a little shade for the drying roots of the grass.

There are sometimes places in some gardens which are difficult and perhaps even dangerous to mow. In my opinion banks and steep slopes should not be put down to grass. They should grow instead some shrubs, if necessary low growing, but certainly thick enough to prevent the growth of grasses and weeds below them. If these should block the view from windows or the driveway, these carpeting shrubs can be used. Thymes, which are extremely varied, can be useful and colourful. Heathers are ideal on acid soil and one or two kinds will tolerate lime. The rose of sharon is a good carpeting shrub that will effectively choke the growth of any weeds below it and not require too much thinning itself. It is sometimes suggested that a chamomile lawn can be made on a bank or steep slope, but I suggest that this might be unwise because chamomile can be extremely slippery underfoot, particularly after rain. Chamomile can certainly be used for sections of a more level lawn and will require less cutting than grass if one of the lower growing, almost flowerless types is grown. A mixture of chamomile and grass can be pleasant and useful, particularly where the soil is of a dry and sandy nature, for chamomile grows well under dry conditions.

It is always well to consider paving areas which are difficult to mow, or using some other surface such as gravel, and then softening these with suitable plants. Most tough rock plants and some silver-leaved kinds are useful. Sometimes one particular portion of lawn becomes worn because of the constant passage of feet, and this is the place where a few paving stones can save a great deal of trouble. There are also the places, as I have mentioned earlier, where for some reason the grass never seems to get cut. Pave these areas and make for yourself a less complicated garden and an easier mind. Remember that gravel or sand can look very well in a garden if kept clean, raked, and weed free. An annual application of a total and long-term weedkiller will ensure that the surface need not be weeded for many months at a time. It is still possible to grow a large tree in an area where all weeds are kept permanently killed by chemical application. The weedkiller will stay in the surface soil and will not damage the deep roots of a mature tree.

## Flowers

There has been a tendency in recent years to dismiss herbaceous flowers from the garden and turn instead to trees and shrubs, the thought behind this tendency being that the larger, longer-lived plants require less attention and so cut labour and energy costs. (I have a friend whose garden is almost filled with shrubs which her husband loves, but so many bring her little pleasure. She cries out for 'real' flowers, in particular foxgloves, sweet williams and delphiniums!)

It is true to a degree that shrubs are labour saving, but any turning away from herbaceous plants is due not so much to any shortcomings of these plants but rather mistakes in the way that they have been selected or used. All plants have their preferences whether to grow in sun or shade, in sandy or clay soil, in an airy or protected site, on limy or acid soil. Most gardeners tend to see a certain plant and admire it because it is growing well. Then, without consideration of the conditions enjoyed by that plant they try to grow it in their own gardens and find it difficult to understand why it fails when it did so well in a friend's plot.

As I have said before, and as I shall doubtless say again, the way to gardening pleasure is to co-operate with the physical conditions of your garden, not to fight them. At the end of this section are one or two lists of perennial plants which prefer to be grown under certain conditions. This is not to say that they will not grow in other places or under other conditions, just that they will normally grow best this way. In my own garden I tend to mix all kinds, as a rule using the shrubs or trees as a background for the herbaceous kinds, although we have one formal straight herbaceous border.

Annual and biennial flowers are easy enough to grow for the most part. The first, if they are hardy, can be sown where they are to bloom, either be sown in autumn when they will flower in early summer, or in spring, when they will flower a little later. Half-hardy annuals are best raised under glass, i.e., indoors or in a cool greenhouse, and given much more attention. These include the 'bedding' plants and their flowering season is longer than that of the hardies. Biennials can be sown outdoors and then either planted out in spaced rows, to await their spaces in border or container when the present tenants have faded, or, if you have a large enough area, some can be left to seed themselves year after year; examples are forget-me-nots, foxgloves, and honesty. These sometimes even become invasive, so you have to pull them up ruthlessly from areas where they are not welcome, or carefully dig them up and pass them to friends.

It is no use turning entirely to perennial herbaceous plants, however, unless they are selected with understanding. A vast amount of time and frustration will be avoided in the garden if only those plants are grown which do not need staking or supporting, although you might then deny yourself such beauties as delphiniums. The trouble is that one can set one's face resolutely in this direction and think that one is fulfilling one's purpose, but then succeed in growing a certain plant so well that it becomes tall and begins to flop and then needs staking. Or another plant may be placed too near to the lawn and so requires propping up to save it from the mower as it passes. Still another plant may perform splendidly in dry weather yet flop with the weight of rain on its leaves. So it is really a counsel of perfection to advise a ban on all plants which are likely to require staking. Nevertheless, by bearing in mind the fact that those with a tendency to require this assistance are likely to cause extra trouble and irritation, one can avoid them to some degree. Otherwise, collect a good supply of strong, twiggy sticks, the pea-stick type, and while the plants are young surround each, or each small group, with these set well into the ground. The young growth will develop upwards and hide, yet be supported by, the sticks. Obviously, use the tallest sticks for the tallest plants and expect the growth to rise a foot or so (30cm) above the sticks.

What, then, is the difference between annuals, biennials, and perennials? Briefly, an annual plant is one that germinates from seed, flowers, and then dies, all in the course of a single year; and a biennial is one that takes two years to do this. A perennial is a little more complex. A hardy herbaceous perennial plant, to give it its full title, is one that will remain alive through the winter, yet one whose leaves, stems, flowers, and other parts above the ground will die back at this time, leaving the root system alive but dormant. The difference between a herbaceous plant and a tree or shrub is that the trunks and stems of the latter are of a woody and permanent nature; and the difference between a herbaceous plant and a bulb, corm, or tuber is simply that these last grow from these sources rather than from roots. So bulbs, etc. can legitimately grow and be classed among hardy herbaceous perennials, not strictly perhaps, but for the sake of simplicity.

A further advantage of hardy herbaceous perennials, hinted at earlier, is that given reasonable care and good fortune (a major factor in making gardening a pleasure as it is with so many things!) the first cost is the last, at least for a number of years. It is not necessary each year to spend money on fresh seed or time on raising new plants. They are already there and the most they ask is rejuvenation by the division of the root system once every three or four years, the choked and elderly centre being discarded and the roots of the remainder prised apart to make several clumps, all of which if planted separately will make splendid and virile new displays.

If the bed or border filled with hardy herbaceous perennials needs no re-stocking each year, it follows that the ground should be clean, rich, and well prepared before planting and that it should be maintained in the same state afterwards. This can be important, and as it is a matter of one single effort, we cannot really begrudge the soil the attention it deserves. The location of the bed or border should be chosen with care, which may seem an obvious thing to say but is still worth saying. I can see no purpose, for example, in making a splendid and colourful herbaceous border which cannot be seen from the house windows, or one where the worst of the wind and bad weather can do great harm, when other locations with better conditions are available. Some spot where the worst of the wind is deflected and where a certain amount of beneficial warmth and light from the sun can have its influence is ideal and is usually fairly easy to find. This is why most of the perennials in my own garden are backed by shrubs, and to ensure that they do not rob each other of the available food the beds are enriched each year.

Whether to make a border or a bed is a matter of personal choice and one which depends to some extent on the facilities available. A straight border at the side or sides, or one with a wavy edge, is usually best in a fairly small garden as it does not interfere with other features, and although perhaps a little obvious, even dull, it is eminently practical and space saving. Where the area available is larger, and particularly where the land undulates gently, island beds are undoubtedly ideal. The arch-priest of island beds, the famous nurseryman Alan Bloom, has shown beyond doubt what can be done with them and has created a pattern of garden making which is possibly the most important change in this direction since Gertrude Jekyll more than half a century ago. And basically there is not a great deal of difference between them, when one understands that Gertrude's borders were made and tended at a time when professional jobbing gardeners were still to be found and could be paid to carry out the constant task of staking those plants at the back of the border and tying in plants to these stakes as they grew in height. Alan, too, has had the advantage of half a century of breeding and selection among plants, so that many of those he chooses are now dwarf, strong-stemmed, and sturdy enough to stand, bright and handsome, in the centre of an island bed without the benefit of the support needed by Gertrude's version of the same plant fifty years before.

But many plants have other vices than merely growing too tall. Some are so strong and confident that they take over a bed, invading the space of more modest blooms, shouldering them aside, dominating them, and adopting an unpleasant and arrogant attitude. Others drop their seed with reckless abandon and young plants soon cover not only whole patches of the bed but appear in all kinds of unsuspected and otherwise engaged places throughout the garden. Both of these types require discipline.

Probably the easiest way to deal with these plants is to keep a wary eye on them once their habits are known, so that the necessary action can be taken before things have gone too far. Parts of some plants can be dug up if they appear to be spreading too far, while others can be pulled up and discarded. Simple dead heading can encourage the faint and the weary to put out more flowers and to prolong their season. Often a little extra plant food for one individual will make the world of difference.

But it is really a matter of choice in the beginning that counts. If the right plants are chosen the results are most likely to be good. Look for sturdy plants. Find out which are those that have a long flowering period, that have a good and attractive appearance before they come into flower, that produce fine flowers over a long period, and which still look pleasant after the flowers have died. And by the way, don't be in too much of a hurry to cut them back when they have faded. Some of our greatest pleasures have come from the birds which have spent hours in autumn and winter perching on certain seed heads or the stalks we left standing. Certainly, if you have heavy clay soil and the accompanying slug pests, do not cut down the stalks until spring. After all, they are not occupying space you would otherwise be using nor are they consuming food and moisture required by other plants.

Weeds can be a nuisance in flower beds and borders, and methods should be sought to suppress them and keep down their numbers. Close planting in the first place is always a help, for where a flower grows a weed cannot. There really is no reason why comparatively large areas of empty soil should be visible in a flower bed, for these areas are a constant invitation to weeds and besides are a waste of good space which should be devoted to flowering plants. It is a good practice also if you see a weed to dig it up and immediately replace it with a flower seedling or a bulb. If herbaceous material grows closely together it always helps to keep down weeds, but at the same time it makes it very difficult to fork lightly around the plants or otherwise inhibit or get rid of what weeds there might be. This is where heavy mulching can play its part, for regular and heavy mulches of peat or some similar moisture retentive material will do much to smother an undergrowth of weeds and to prevent their seeds from germinating. But remember that peat, excellent though it may be in the garden, does not have any nutritive value and must therefore be supplemented by a fertilizer. The best way to do this is to apply a sprinkling of fertilizer at the recommended dosage around each plant, fork this in very lightly, and then to dress the area with moist peat. The latter will help the former to get down to the roots where it will do the most good.

The following lists give the names of perennial plants particularly suited to certain conditions. It will be found that some are listed under several labels, which only indicates how versatile and useful they are. Not all varieties are the same, so check if possible.

*Dry conditions*
Achillea                              Anaphalis

Anthemis
Aquilegia
Artemisia
Bergenia
Catananche
Cephalaria
Epimedium
Geranium

Hypericum
Lamium
Pachysandra
Polygonum
Saxifraga
Solidago
Vinca

*Moist conditions*
Aconitum
Ajuga
Astilbe
Cimicifuga
Digitalis
Hemerocallis
Hosta
Lobelia
Lithrum
Mimulus

Monarda
Primula
Pulmonaria
Ranunculus
Rudbeckia
Salvia
Senecio
Solidago
Trollius

*Windy and open conditions*
Agapanthus
Alyssum
Anemone
Armeria
Artemisia
Bergenia
Centaurea
Echinops
Euphorbia
Geranium
Hemerocallis

Kniphofia
Lathyrus
Limonium
Nepeta
Potentilla
Santolina
Scabiosa
Sedum
Stachys
Tradescantia
Yucca

*Growing well on clay*
Aconitum
Ajuga
Aster
Astilbe
Caltha

Campanula
Cephalaria
Digitalis
Doronicum
Erigeron

Euphorbia
Gentiana
Geranium
Hemerocallis
Hosta
Iris
Ligularia
Lysimachia
Lythrum

Physalis
Primula
Ranunculus
Rudbeckia
Salvia
Saponaria
Solidago
Tradescantia

*Accepting sun and drought*

Acanthus
Achillea
Allium
Alstroemeria
Alyssum
Anaphalis
Anchusa
Anthemis
Artemisia
Campanula
Caryopteris
Catananche
Centaurea
Ceratostigma
Crinum
Dianthus
Dictamnus
Echinops
Eryngium
Euphorbia

Gypsophila
Hypericum
Kniphofia
Lavandula
Linaria
Lupin
Nepeta
Nerine
Oxalis
Paeonia
Papaver
Phlomis
Polygonum
Potentilla
Pyrethrum
Santolina
Scabiosa
Stachys
Verbascum
Verbena

*Growing on chalk*

Acanthus
Aconitum
Allium
Alyssum
Anthemis
Artemisia
Campanula

Catananche
Centaurea
Clematis
Dianthus
Digitalis
Doronicum
Echinops

Eryngium
Gaillardia
Galega
Gypsophila
Hemerocallis
Hypericum
Iris
Lathyrus
Lavandula
Linaria

Nepeta
Paeonia
Papaver
Pulmonaria
Pyrethrum
Scabiosa
Sedum
Tradescantia
Verbascum
Veronica

*For ground cover*
Ajuga
Alchemilla
Anaphalis
Antenaria
Bergenia
Dianthus
Epimedium
Festuca
Geranium
Heuchera
Hosta

Hypericum
Lamium
Mimulus
Origanum
Oxalis
Polygonum
Pulmonaria
Santolina
Stachys
Veronica
Vinca

*Strong growers or spreaders, useful, but beware!*
Alyssum
Artemisia
Aster
Bergenia
Centaurea
Cephalaria
Ceratostigma
Echinops
Galega
Geranium
Helianthemum
Lamium

Lavatera
Monarda
Physalis
Polygonum
Rheum
Rudbeckia
Salvia
Saponaria
Solidago
Verbascum
Vinca

Probably because so many of them bloom so prettily during the short days, both in autumn and winter, flowering bulbs (under which umbrella term some corms and tubers are generally grouped for the sake of convenience) bring great pleasure to the gardener. Many of them, especially the small kinds and species of some of the better known types, can be left in the soil year after year. These need not be dead-headed either, as tulips, daffodils, and hyacinths should, but can be allowed to set and drop seed. This is the way in which the ground becomes carpeted with such flowers. Obviously one should select the right site for these kinds, and as they flower so early they often can go below and between trees and shrubs. You can also have them growing up through some ground cover such as low-growing heathers if you wish.

Some people who like an ordered seasonal routine prefer to lift large types such as narcissi and tulips, which may have filled a bed in spring, to replace them with summer flowering plants; in this case the bulbs need not be wasted, but simply heeled in somewhere so that they can continue fading naturally, after which time the bulbs can be cleaned, stored in a dry place, and replanted later. However, if you wish to save work, you can plant them in groups among shrubs and other perennial herbaceous plants. Alternatively you can inter-plant the spring flowering kinds with biennials, even those which can be left to seed themselves if you wish, such as forget-me-not and honesty. Or you can grow biennials such as wallflowers, brompton stocks, and double daisies easily and cheaply from seed simply for this purpose. These companion plants will not only enhance the beauty of the bulb flowers, but will mask them as they die down. It is best to allow the bulb leaves to die naturally rather than cut them off. If you grow wallflowers or brompton stocks, you can be sure also of adding to the scents in the garden.

Autumn bulbs are often overlooked, but given a warm, sheltered border you can grow such beauties as amaryllis and nerines, which flower from late August to October and sometimes longer. There are also sternbergia and a number of true autumn crocuses and colchicums which can be grown like the spring kinds.

Fragrance is essential in a pleasure garden. There are many hardy lilies and most grow magnificently in borders. If, though, you garden as we do in the depths of the countryside, you may find that the bulbs gradually disappear, as they obviously form part of some creature's diet. We have overcome this difficulty by growing lilies in pots which we stand on the paved areas near the house, where we can enjoy their fragrance. There is no reason, if you have to resort to this method, why you should not wait until they are almost ready to bloom and then stand the pots in among other plants in the border where they will be masked and the flowers will be on display, and then remove them later so that you can take care of the bulbs.

If until now the only bulbs you have tended to think of are crocuses daffodils, tulips, and hyacinths, do send for a catalogue from one of the many good bulb merchants who deal in mail order. It is possible to find enough kinds to have some in flower outdoors all the year round, and failing catastrophe these should all increase as the years go by.

### Trees and Shrubs

There are a great many trees and shrubs suitable for gardens of all kinds, large and small, open and sheltered, acid or alkaline, on heavy or light soil. There are trees and shrubs with gorgeous flowers and with distinctive foliage, some heavily perfumed, some tall, and some spreading. There is a shrub flower for every month of the year.

There is no doubt in my mind that the best way for a gardener to choose shrubs and trees for his own plot is to go to a famous garden, to an arboretum or a botanic garden, and in some instances to a nursery, and see them actually growing. No amount of catalogue description and no photographs can ever give the real impression of the growing plant. See them not only as you will plant them, young, small, and immature, but as they will eventually grow, large, spreading, covered in blossom, thick with leaves. Note any that particularly take your fancy and try to picture this actual tree in location in your own garden. Ask yourself if it will fit, grow too tall, too wide, whether it will blend well with its neighbours. Make sure that your own soil and general conditions are compatible with the needs of the plant, and if not, don't try to grow it unless you are genuinely prepared to devote time and money to it, and even then still probably lose it in the long run.

Expert gardeners tell us repeatedly never to plant trees and shrubs too close to each other. Find the eventual spread of two neighbouring trees, we are advised, add these figures, divide by two and take this as your planting distance. In other words, if you wish to plant a tall, slim conifer with a total mature spread, width or thickness of 10ft (3m) next to a turkey oak with a mature span of 20ft (6m), then add these two figures together and divide the result by two to find your correct planting distance, in this case 15ft (4½m).

So with our brand new and embarrassingly naked garden we go out with two trees, carefully measure their planting distances, and put them into soil. To our dismay we find that they can hardly be seen. They are so small and insignificant that they seem to play no part in furnishing or decorating the garden. We will have to wait ten years or more before either plays its proper role. So in disgust or desperation we plant two or three trees in the vacant space between our original two and find that we now have the beginnings of a sensible shrub border. And if we do this we may be laying up a store of trouble for ourselves.

The answer to this very real problem, I think, is to divide your garden plantings of trees and shrubs into permanent and temporary. The permanent trees should go in at the correct spacing, for then they will grow without obstruction or damage to themselves. Between them smaller trees and shrubs can be planted, less important though perhaps just as attractive. Look on these as present pleasures, quite clearly stop gaps, either to be moved after a few years, or to be destroyed or perhaps dug up and presented to some gardener friend. Some can be moved quite successfully and without great trouble, if they have not yet reached a state of maturity.

This advice can involve considerable expenditure, it is true, and this can be lessened somewhat if the gaps are filled with herbaceous plants, even annuals, rather than other shrubs. There is a wide range of herbaceous material which goes well in conjunction with more woody growth, and a further advantage here is that herbaceous plants are easier and quicker to move. May I suggest, however, that if the cost of shrubby plants, daunting at first, is spread over the ten years or so of their useful life as a mere stop gap, then it would appear more reasonable and less frightening than it first seemed. All trees and shrubs should be costed on their useful life, in which case the price of some is so low as to be almost incredible.

When the trees are first planted there is some allied cost, perhaps for peat, fertilizer, a stake, and a tie or two. The cost of these small items can reach a sizeable total if a number of plantings are to be made. But once again, look at the expenditure on these plants in the years to come. A light spread of bonemeal or some other fertilizer around the base once a year. The stake and the tie will probably be unnecessary after the first few years and can be removed for use elsewhere. So what other cost is there? Only a share of the cost of spade and hoe, rake and pruners, plus the time and energy expended.

No matter how desperately you have always longed for a certain tree, pause before you buy it. Do remember that the growth and spread of trees and shrubs in the garden affect not only neighbouring trees and shrubs, they can also affect such things as buildings, walls and fences, paths and driveways and neighbours; so these matters should always be taken into account when making any plantings. Many of us have seen, with wry amusement, a pretty little weeping willow planted in a new suburban front lawn just before the dining room window. Of course it looks charming and the view from the house must be highly gratifying. But before ten years are out it will be found necessary to trim the tree to let in some light. To trim a weeping willow and still keep it attractive in appearance requires considerable skill, so after an increasingly disgruntled year or two it becomes apparent that the tree will have to come out. This is a great shame, a great waste of time, money, energy, and sheer delight.

Often another new gardener plants his weeping willow in the garden to overhang the pretty little fish pool he had so laboriously built. Here he discovers two things: the leaves shadow the pool so that plants fail to grow properly, and the leaves as they fall kill the fish, for the willow (*Salix*) is a source of salicin, which eventually was synthesized into acetylsalicylic acid, or aspirin.

How many of us have been irritated by having to stoop below a low branch when walking down the garden path to the shed, or have had to bend dangerously with the mower for the same reason? How many lawns are improperly mown simply because the branches of some tree or shrub lie in the way of the mower? How many of us have suddenly noticed with astonishment that out of the centre of some bushy shrub is arising the grown crown of an oak, an ash, or even a hornbeam, developing from some accidentally deposited seed unseen and unnoticed until of a startling size? All these things happen because we are not paying attention to the trees and shrubs in our garden. We expect them to look after themselves and so they do, admirably; but even an unused room requires dusting occasionally.

One of the things that sometimes goes unnoticed until a real problem has been created is the appearance of sucker growth around the roots of a tree or shrub. This may not matter if the plant is growing on its own roots instead of being grafted on to the roots of some more vigorous plant except that the suckers may spoil the overall shape, but if the plant, is grafted it is imperative that the suckers be removed as early as possible. Follow them down through the soil to where they arise from the root and cut them away cleanly at this point. If this is not done there is a real danger that they may take the plant over. Roses and lilac are particularly prone to suckering, as are some viburnums, rhododendrons, and azaleas, and what happens is that you are left with a dog rose, a privet, or some undistinguished plant. Heavy mulching around the roots of the plants will help to keep down suckers and if they are found while young they can usually be killed quite safely by spraying with paraquat.

In the same way that suckers can take over a plant and overcome the particular characteristics that make it special, so some trees and shrubs with an exceptional foliage colour or variegation will sometimes send out a branch which has reverted to the original plain green. Allow enough time to be quite certain that this is so and then prune this branch right back to the main trunk, otherwise there is a strong likelihood that it will take over and the tree or shrub will lose its special characteristic.

The pruning of ornamental trees and shrubs is a vexed question, and I must admit to being biased personally. I will prune a tree or shrub only if I know it to be necessary or if it is being a nuisance. I prefer to let them go their own way as a general rule, for I can look from my own garden up the hill to the woods and see thousands of splendid trees and shrubs all of which are doing well and looking wonderful without benefit of any pruning or shaping other than that given by the wind and by one to the other. Yet I realize and accept that roses, to take one example of a flowering shrub, will give more and better flowers if I prune them at least once a year to induce strong growth and the production of flower buds. But even here I sometimes prune less vigorously than is approved by some of the experts, preferring to allow a more natural growth and to take a second bite at the cake when I collect flowers for indoor decoration, making a cut just above a bud pointing in the right direction as a kind of summer pruning. Most of my shrubs are pruned this way also. I select the curved, ungainly, even weakly and crossing stems and cut these right back to the location of good growth.

Many shrubs, perhaps even most of the shrubs we grow in our gardens, need no regular pruning and require cutting back only when they exceed their allotted space, when they have been damaged or when frost or snow has killed or wounded certain parts. If a plant has grown too large, do not snip little pieces off branches to get it back to a convenient size, for as a rule this will encourage the growth of new shoots and so nullify your work. Instead, cut away a whole branch right back to the main stem. As a rule this should be done in winter while the plant is dormant. Don't consign this branch to the bonfire though, for divided properly, it may do for taking or supporting perennials and other plants in the spring. There may also be some good, straight stems on it which will make hardwood cuttings.

Some shrubs definitely benefit from regular pruning. These are grown for the flowers they produce. But we must be careful, for some develop their flowers in the current year's growth and some on growth made in the previous year. Careless cutting can result in the loss of the season's blooms. Some of the shrubs that produce their flowers on the previous year's growth include forsythias, winter jasmine, kerria, philadelphus, some spirea, and weigela. As soon as their flowers have faded, the branches that held them should be cut away. New shoots will begin to grow almost immediately and will then have an opportunity to develop and mature during the forthcoming summer so as to produce a good flower crop in the next season.

Among those shrubs that produce their flowers on the current year's growth are buddleia, caryopteris, many escallonias and hardy fuchsias, most of the hypericums, the lovely and so easy to grow *Leycesteria formosa*, the golden leaved sambucus or elder, and the feathery tamarisk. Cut away the old shoots that have flowered at almost any mild part of the winter unless you live in a very cold area, in which case it is best to wait until the beginning of spring. As a rule, cut the shoots down to a single bud or to an alternate pair of good, plump buds.

There are also one or two plants such as members of the willow and dogwood families which are grown largely because of their vivid stem colour in the winter, brilliant reds, oranges, yellows, and greens. These brightly coloured stems are the young growth only and to induce their growth the plants should be cut down almost to ground level at the beginning of summer.

One of the major reasons why trees and shrubs are as a general rule extremely labour saving in a garden is that most are almost free from pest and disease attack unless they are old or infirm. This indicates to us that when these plants have passed their best, often they should be removed and replaced with a younger specimen. Some will tolerate a severe cutting back, but much of the success of this operation will depend upon the season. Some trees and shrubs, particularly modern hybrids which are grown because of their exceptionally heavy flowering, early flowering, leaf colour, or some other unusually attractive habit of growth, have a much shorter life than is generally believed, sometimes as little as ten years or so. When a tree or shrub of this nature fails to put in a good performance one year it should be watched carefully and if it fails in the succeeding year it should be removed in case it spreads to other plants in the locality some disease that has hit it simply because it has become old.

Aphid and caterpillar attack can disfigure and harm some trees and shrubs, and where this is so one of the many normal garden insecticides can be used. On the other hand, if your garden is as full of birds, ladybirds, and other predators as it ought to be, you can usually leave it to them to keep down attacks of this nature. Actually it works both ways, for it will help you to have insects kept under control by the birds and it helps the birds to feed their young and increase in numbers if they find a ready source of food in the form of aphids and caterpillars on the plants.

Trees and shrubs are marketed in two ways, either container-grown or lifted from the open ground. The difference is significant, in price, in convenience, and in helpfulness to the new or unpractised gardener.

Container-grown plants are normally available at garden centres. As the term suggests, the plants are growing in a container of some kind, perhaps a flower pot, a plastic sleeve, a fibre pot, or even a large preserve tin or can. Every reputable retailer will sell only plants which have actually been growing in their containers for a period of at least several months, rather than plants which have been hurriedly stuffed into a pot of some kind only a few days before being offered for sale. The longer a plant has been growing in its pot, within reason, the bigger and better will be its root system, so when planted out into the soil of your garden this vigorous root system will ensure strong, steady, and early growth.

The benefits of container-grown plants are mainly that in the first place they can be examined, inspected carefully for any damage, disease or insect attack, appraised as an addition to the garden while in full leaf and even full flower, and taken away in your own transport for planting at a time convenient to you. Secondly, they can be planted at any time of the year, even full summer, so long as the primary precautions have been taken. This means that with a new garden it is perfectly possible to go to a nursery or garden centre on a Saturday morning and select and bring home the trees, shrubs, and herbaceous plants that have caught your eye. In the afternoon and on the succeeding Sunday you can dig the necessary holes and put in your plants. By the beginning of Monday your garden will already be furnished and ready to go.

Everything good must be paid for and it is inevitable that container-grown plants should be more expensive than those lifted from the open ground. Remember that the producer has had to pot his plants in successively larger containers over a period sometimes of years before they are ready for sale. This involves a high proportion of skilled labour, which must be paid for. The nurseryman or garden centre proprietor is saving you time and labour and for this you must pay. And apart from the cost, other disadvantages of container grown plants are that one must look very carefully to see that the plants you buy are, in fact, container *grown* and not merely container *marketed*. Be certain that they have been watered well. The container should be full of good roots. If you are suspicious, ask to see the roots, which should be many, vigorous, strong, and looking almost as if they were bursting to get out of the container. The soil around them should be just moist, not wet. A garden centre or a nursery with an established reputation is your best guarantee. To established gardeners one of the main disadvantages of container-grown plants is that often there is a very limited choice. As is only to be expected, a grower will produce only those plants he knows he will sell, those which are popular and to be seen in almost every garden. He might grow a rare and prized specimen in a container and have it on his hands, costing him money in space and attention, for many years and then finally have to plant it out in his own grounds rather than have it die, its roots too confined in the comparatively small container over this long period. Yet on the other hand one occasionally finds nurseries which specialize in unusual plants.

The root system of container-grown plants should be maintained in its neat ball or pack when they are planted out in your garden. Sometimes it is possible to slip the plant neatly out of its pot leaving the root ball intact, but for larger specimens it will usually be found necessary to split, cut, or crack the container. Estimate the necessary size of the planting hole before removing the plant from its container, allowing just an extra inch or two of depth and diameter for the addition of fresh soil. This should ideally be a mixture of good soil with compost, well-rotted farmyard manure, or moist peat with the addition of a handful of bonemeal or some similar slow-acting fertilizer. This should be directed into the planting hole underneath the root ball of the new plant and around the sides so that the plant is held firmly and the soil level is identical with the top of the root ball. Firm the new soil by treading so that it is roughly the same texture or solidity as the root ball. Where a stake is necessary, fix this firmly and securely in the hole before planting and secure the new plant to it carefully.

If the weather is warm and sunny and if there is a strong wind, make sure that the plant is never allowed to dry out during its first month or so of life in your care. Water the soil thoroughly and sprinkle the foliage each evening if possible, preferably with rain water. The plant should get away quickly and put out its strong roots into the surrounding soil. New growth at the extremities of the roots will be an indication that it is growing well and is in good health.

As a general rule growth will be slow for the first two years while the plant sends out its roots and becomes accustomed to its new home. Not until the third year will significant new growth be seen and this should be maintained in the years to come.

Trees and shrubs lifted from the open ground by a nurseryman are a matter for his own convenience rather than your own. He will advise you when you may expect to receive your plants, invariably some time between October and about March, so that you can make the necessary arrangements for their planting. When he lifts them, the conscientious nurseryman will protect their roots with soil, moss, straw or some similar material and wrap or ball them carefully. The parcel you receive by mail or by carrier will be beautifully packed and prepared and it is a rare matter for there to be any damage in transit.

When your plants arrive, remove the stem wrappings and stand the plants in a cold, dry place, perhaps with some extra protection for their roots, which must never be allowed to dry out. Never try to plant when the ground is frosted or when it is wet and waterlogged. If weather or other activities prevent you planting your trees or shrubs for some days, you will be advised to heel them in, a simple operation which involves the digging of a trench in the soil some 1ft (30cm) or so deep and as long as necessary. The plants are stood in this trench leaning against one of the sides and the soil is then returned, to be spread over the roots. The plants will remain here quite happily for some weeks, although obviously the sooner they are properly planted in their permanent positions the better they will be, for otherwise there is the danger that stems which should be straight might become curved or misshapen, and the root growth might begin prematurely.

If you plant more or less immediately, try to prepare your planting holes in advance and have ready everything you will need. Place the stake in position and make sure it is firm and steady before you insert your plant into the hole. Keep the plant roots out of the drying wind or the sun until you are ready for planting. It often pays to stand the roots in a bucket of water for an hour or two before planting so that they can absorb some of the moisture they may have lost through being out of the soil for some days. If the weather is very dry and the leaves are wilting, and particulaily in the case of conifers, it can be helpful to spray the entire plant with a substance known simply as S600. This forms a light waxy coating over the leaf surfaces and prevents transpiration for a week or two. It wears off by itself after this time.

Make sure that the mark on the stem of the plant indicating where the soil level was previously is again at soil level, neither above nor below. Make sure also that the soil sifted into the planting hole on top of the roots is well tramped down and that no air pockets exist. Shake the plant gently from time to time as the new soil is sifted in as this will help to settle it around the roots and firm it down as you work, finishing off by pressing down on the soil firmly with the heel of the foot to make sure that all is well compacted. Fix in position the tie on to the stake so that the plant cannot rock with the wind. Water thoroughly and make sure for the first month or so that the soil around the roots is never allowed to become dry, although of course neither should it become waterlogged. Try always to use rain water, because tap or well water is likely to carry a heavier concentration of lime or other chemicals in it than will normally be tolerated by certain calcifuges and in any case rain water is a more natural product.

### Fruit and Vegetables

Tremendous interest has been shown in the growing of fruit and vegetables in recent years. This is partly because of the economic situation, as prices in the shops have risen steeply and significant economies can be made by growing your own. But this is not the only reason. The greater benefits of vitamin-rich foods, the better flavour, the extra convenience of having freshly-picked food crops regularly to hand, the advantages of being able to deep freeze or otherwise store or preserve food crops for use during winter, the ability to plan a continual supply, a general conscience about conservation, ecology, world shortages, and the like – all these things play a part in the greater interest in food growing.

Even the smallest garden can grow some food crops. Indeed, a garden is not necessary, for herbs, carrots, lettuces, tomatoes, radish, and even potatoes can be grown in pots on a window-sill. It is true that little significant contribution to world food shortages will be achieved this way, but the provision of fresh and home-grown vegetables even for a single meal will still be worth while. In a really small garden it is not necessary to have a definite section or area put aside for the growing of fruit and vegetables. It may be impossible to grow large quantities, but where space is limited some crops, such as tomatoes and cucumbers, can be grown against a sunny wall, the occasional lettuce will grow well and happily among the flowers (I've seen them edging a rose bed), carrots will look attractive at the base of shrubs, and perpetual and alpine strawberries will make a pretty edging to a flower border. For this purpose choose vegetables which can be cut off at ground level or simply pulled up when required, so that the flower roots are not unduly disturbed. There is no reason why you should not make a mixed vegetable border along the side of a path, just as you would make one of flowers. You can make an edging of herbs such as thyme, parsley, and chives. You can divide the border into 10ft long (3m) sections, filling each with something new as the first crop is used, such as lettuce sown in autumn, eaten in spring, followed by courgette. One section can take spinach, one a block of sweet corn, one baby carrots, another baby beets or dwarf beans, with a row of tomatoes or tripods of climbing beans or cucumbers at the back. There is really no limit, and although I have a large vegetable garden of my own, I also have 10ft strips (3m) where I can experiment in this way and I can assure you that it works.

Obviously, it is best wherever possible to set aside a special plot for the cultivation of fruit and vegetables, and it will pay to take this seriously enough at the outset to enclose this area with wire netting and fix a scaffolding to allow a net roof to be pulled over at some parts of the year. This will ensure that the crops you grow will be yours instead of being taken by birds or animals, and it will also help psychologically by instilling the feeling that this particular plot is one that will be producing material of genuine importance and value. It is interesting to note that an enclosed fruit cage of this type also provides sufficient protection to raise internal temperatures just that important degree or two.

To grow fruit and vegetables well it is necessary that they should grow quickly and lushly. This way they will be tender, fully flavoured, and rich in vitamins. And to grow quickly vegetables need a rich and moist soil. The plot should be chosen with care. It should be in the sun, without overshadowing trees or buildings. It should be protected from the north and east, from the coldest and strongest of winds. It should be convenient to sources of water and, where possible, it should have nearby a 'power house' where are stored fertilizers, peat, compost, all the necessary tools, and where boxes or pots of plants can be stood before planting out in their normal rows under the fruit cage.

Vegetable growing means intensive growing. In your plot you should aim to make use of every inch of soil both to get the greatest possible amount of produce and to take every advantage of the treatment you have given to your soil. My own theory is that if ground covers work in the ornamental garden, they should work in the vegetable plot, and weeds should be suppressed in this manner. The soil should be dug in the first place as deeply and as well as you have time and energy for, and at the same time it should have incorporated into it quantities of such beneficial materials as compost farmyard manure, and enriched peat. Once the plot is filled with growing crops it will never again be possible (nor, in my opinion, necessary) to subject it to such intensive preparation, and a good start is therefore important. Do not use any artificial fertilizers at this stage. They can be expensive and because they give quick and concentrated results they are better used later, as a direct incentive and assistance to young plants when they are in their rows in the soil.

It is often advocated that a vegetable plot should be divided into three, perhaps four, sections and the crops in these sections varied each year. Called the rotation of crops, this technique can prove helpful but it is not essential. The idea behind it is that some crops need a great deal of fertilizer to do well, other need less. Some crops travel deeply into the soil and others do little more than sit on the surface. Obviously, because intensive cultivation results in the production of large quantities of food crops which are removed from the plot into the kitchen, the soil becomes more and more depleted of its richness as this process continues, and means must be found of replacing the goodness that has been taken out. Some plants deposit certain chemicals into the soil which in time will poison other crops if allowed to build up, so it is helpful to move these crops around to lessen this concentration. Other crops can deposit such useful products as nitrogen into the soil, and a rotation of crops will allow others to benefit from this.

Those who believe rotation necessary suggest, for instance, that in the first year one section of the plot might be put down to potatoes, followed by spring cabbage, broccoli, and leeks. In the second year the same section will grow spring onions, lettuces, radishes, tomatoes, and the like, followed this time by brussels sprouts, cauliflowers, and savoy cabbages. Finally, in the third year, the plot will hold spinach, peas, beans, turnips and parsnips, beetroots and carrots.

By adopting a cycle such as this there is one section of the plot free, in other words left empty, each winter, to be double dug and carefully enriched by the addition of compost, farmyard manure, or some similar material, so that the soil is regularly revitalized after its intensive cultivation.

It all makes sense and for those with space, time, and energy plus an orderly and virtuous mind, the practice is sound and beneficial. But with those of us with too little space to leave any of it vacant for any part of the year, for those of us who find little enough time for the garden even when we cut down on recommended gardening practices, for those of us who prefer our gardening to be a pleasure and a relaxation rather than the grim and urgent following of careful plans, then I suggest that it is really unnecessary, so long as the soil we work is kept at all times in as good condition as is compatible with low cost and low labour. Personally I accept the sense of the rotation of crops by following a top crop with a root crop, usually as soon as the first crop is out of the ground. If the location of the various vegetables is changed year by year, much of the qualities of a strict rotation will be observed and much of the rewards gained without spending too much space, time, and energy on activities which may be ideal but are certainly not necessary.

But there is also another matter to be taken into consideration, or rather there is a series of matters. The 'rules' for double digging, bastard trenching, the rotation of crops, and other hallowed vegetable growing traditions were first laid down many years ago and have merely been repeated through the years because they are the ideal. But they are the ideal only because at that time there was plenty of cheap labour available. Even a modest home with a garden was able to maintain a man and a boy to work on the plot. Again, families in those days were large, for not only were there more children in the family, but grandmother and maiden aunt, cook and servants helped to swell the numbers. So the production of quantities of food crops was essential.

Today the number of people per house is smaller. The garden is smaller. There is no outside labour to be had or even afforded. This means that we require smaller quantities of food and at the same time, because we are more demanding in our tastes, we prefer our vegetables to be small, young, and tender rather than large. Because space and time are limited we sometimes cut out those crops which demand much space and which are freely available in the shops, and grow instead foods which are difficult or expensive to buy or which taste so much better when pulled or cut straight from the garden and brought into the kitchen.

All of this helps to show that the old practices do not necessarily apply today and that instead we have gained a new virtue and a new technique: the intensive growing of a constant succession of crops. Because land is scarce and gardens are small we must make the best possible use of every square foot. There is no excuse for bare soil among the vegetables. If seed has been sown and one must wait for the crop to appear, then sow in the same row, or perhaps in the space between rows, a catch crop of, say, radish, although this space also can sometimes be used as a nursery area for seedlings, lettuce for example, which can later be transplanted to another place. Sowing radish in a row will help you in two ways, for it will show you exactly where the slowly germinating seed is and it will be ready for pulling and clearing by the time the main crop seed is appearing through the soil. So you are getting two crops at the same time from the same piece of soil, surely a practice just as virtuous as double digging.

Intensive cropping of this kind does necessitate a really rich soil and one that is in good condition. So plenty of humus-making materials must be added constantly. These include garden compost, well decayed farmyard manure, peat, even lawn mowings. Fork these into the top inches of the soil or merely spread them generously on the surface and let the worms drag them down. They will decay, aid bacterial activity, and help release into the soil the basic chemicals absorbed by your plant roots. Remember though to apply lime for members of the cabbage family.

Remember, too, that these basic chemicals absorbed by plant roots must be in liquid solution. This means that plenty of moisture must be available in the soil, even in the driest periods. Mulches of humus-making materials spread thickly on a moist soil will do much to retain soil moisture, but every kitchen garden should have immediately available a constant source of water. Even a rain barrel is a help, so long as it is clearly understood that when watering by hand it is useless to apply less than a couple of gallons (10 litres) to each sq yd (1m²) of soil. To sprinkle on less is merely to wet the surface and is of no benefit of any kind to the crop it holds. All vegetables are comprised very largely of water and if they do not get enough they will be small, tough, and stringy. If your soil is in good condition there should be no likelihood of flooding or drowning your plants, although water should always be applied gently, that is, through a rose, in case some of the smaller seeds might be washed from the soil.

There are one or two crops in the vegetable garden which are more or less permanent. They stay in the ground for years, cropping regularly in their seasons and because of their nature incapable of being moved until or unless they have grown so old and so tired that they should be removed and replaced. Rhubarb and asparagus are examples of these crops. They require little attention other than the application of manure or fertilizer at the beginning of each year. What is important is that these permanent crops should be grown in a location where they will not be a nuisance. So give them a special place where they will not be in the way.

Whereas vegetables can quite easily be lumped together and treated in much the same way, one cannot do the same with fruit, which varies more widely, for there are such fruits as apples, pears, plums, cherries, and peaches, others such as red, white, and black currants, and still others such as blackberries, loganberries and raspberries, and yet another group such as the strawberries.

Only comparatively large gardens can hope to grow quantities of fruit in a special area, for many of them are expensive of space. Most of us have to fit them in with the assortment of other plants we grow. There are today tree or bush fruits which have been grafted on to dwarfing roots, which means that they will never grow very large yet will produce good crops. There are means of growing some plants in a space-saving manner, as cordons, fan-trained against a wall, as a hedge or fence, as the edging to a vegetable or even a flower bed. But space is required and it is usually necessary to make a careful and considered choice rather than try to grow many varied crops, such as one would in the vegetable plot.

The tree fruits such as apples and pears can well be treated as decorative, where space in the garden is limited. This means that they can be planted in the grass or in a border. They will give blossom in season and can be a useful means of furnishing the garden. Seek the advice of your nurseryman when you buy your trees and make sure that they will grow well in your soil and that they are either self-fertile or will have another tree nearby which will help to carry out the necessary pollination. Remember that even self-fertile types generally give better crops if a pollinator is nearby. Your neighbour's tree may do if you have no room for another of your own, so check what this is.

Some fruits require more than average nitrogen in their fertilizer, while others require more than average phosphates, but all require a rich, well-drained soil, and, once established, little or no digging around the roots. Regular applications of heavy mulches at the base of the trees or bushes will encourage earthworm activity and hence a well-drained soil. Roots should never be allowed to get dry.

Pruning can affect cropping but it must be carried out carefully and correctly. If you do not know how to prune, don't do it at all, for you will then get a much better crop than if you prune incorrectly. The intention should be the encouragement of fruit bearing buds at the expense of those which will merely bear leaves. The techniques vary from crop to crop, and it is well to obtain advice from your supplier when you buy your young plants. Pruning may also be necessary to keep trees or bushes to a reasonable size or to the required shape. Stone fruits should not be pruned beyond having dead wood removed.

All fruit crops are subject to the attentions of predators. These can vary from mice to birds and even small girls and boys, and if the garden is left untended or unoccupied for considerable periods it is wise at the appropriate time to discourage the attentions, particularly of birds, or to protect the crop by means of temporary or permanent netting.

All food crops also invite insect attack, although not to the extent where there must be a constant application of insecticides. Well-grown crops are strong and can often shrug off attacks which can kill or seriously distort weak plants. Aphids and caterpillars are easily enough seen and can be dealt with promptly by spraying with one of the various preparations available. Never use any insecticide unless you have to and always use the safest you can, making certain that it is the correct one, that it is applied correctly at the correct time, and that the correct interval is allowed between spraying and harvesting.

Diseases of fruits are generally funguses and are frequently brought by insects or by careless pruning. Fungicides should be used where they are suitable and these can often be used as preventatives rather than cures. It is always advisable, for example, to spray peach trees before the buds open to prevent the disfiguring peach leaf curl, and outdoor tomatoes should be sprayed against blight before they are in fact attacked, particularly when the season is wet and humid. These sprayings should be a regular programme, treated as important as watering and feeding.

If you are a small family a token fruit garden is often sufficient to bring pleasure and satisfaction. A bush each of white, red, and black currants, a short row of raspberries, a fan-trained morello cherry and a loganberry, both of which will grow on north-facing walls or fences if you have no others, a border of strawberries, and a mulberry tree in the courtyard or on the edge of the lawn, all these will take little space. If you have the time and enjoy the disciplines of pruning and training, you can learn about growing fruits on the cordon system and perhaps train two pear trees to make an arch over the garden path, or gooseberries against the inside of the fruit cage. If you want inspiration ask for a fruit catalogue. You will be surprised at the varieties available and the ways they can be grown.

# 5

## AIDS TO EASY GARDENING

Under this label it is possible to introduce the widest range of products, materials, and even skills. One particular aid, for example, is a strong muscular frame and another is a well-watered site. But one must stop somewhere, and it is therefore suggested that tools and chemicals used for the cultivation or treatment of the soil and the plants it holds are probably the best subjects for discussion here, with a glance at such allied subjects as watering appliances, paving and walling materials, greenhouses, propagating cases, cloches, soil warming, and the like.

### Garden Tools
Basic to all gardening are the tools one uses to cultivate the soil. Most of these are hand tools and they are comparatively few in number. They are well known and do not require description, but it might be helpful to suggest which are important, even essential. A spade probably comes first, with a fork a close second, although speaking for myself I use a fork much more often than a spade. Also essential are a hoe, a rake, a trowel, a pair of secateurs, and a pair of hedge clippers or trimmers. These are essential tools for an average garden. Additions can include such aids as a wheelbarrow of some kind (though you might be surprised at how useful a large, strong square of plastic can be for the transport of certain materials), lawn edge-trimmers with long handles, a saw, long-handled pruners, and sharp-tined cultivators.

Buy always the best hand tools you can afford, a sentence easy enough to write but an instruction more difficult to comply with, because one cannot always find a wide choice and because one cannot always see the benefit in spending twice as much for one product as for another almost identical. Look for stainless steel, real stainless steel, not a material said to be 'rustproof' or 'rust resistant'. Handle the tools before you buy them to make sure that they feel comfortable and well balanced in your grip. Never buy a large or a wide spade or fork in preference to a smaller one, under the impression that by this means you will be able to shift more soil in less time. You won't. You will merely become increasingly tired and you may strain your back or some other muscles. Aim to have tools which are light to handle so that you can work easily and comfortably.

When you have brought your tools home find a good place for them. The best place is a special garden shed where you can keep all your tools, your machines such as mowers, your lime and fertilizers, and all the many materials one uses when gardening. Some people are able to use one wall or side area of a garage. Racks on the wall are a good way both of keeping your tools conveniently to hand and saving space in any area. If you keep them always in the same place you will be able to see at a glance if anything is missing, probably left at the site of some task or lying in the grass, and you can quickly go in search of it.

After you have used any tool try always to clean it of soil or sap and wipe it over lightly with an oily rag. This way you will keep your tools always ready for use and prolong their lives. Try, too, to keep them sharp. A spade with a sharp edge is much easier to use than one which has been allowed to become blunt. A quick rub over with a suitable file or a stone is all that is necessary. Good tools keep a sharp edge longer than those made from inferior metals, and the handle of a spade, say, will break less readily, will be smoother to the hands, more easily seen in the bushes, if it is composed of some brightly coloured, plastic-covered metallic alloy than heavier, water absorbent, easily splintered wood.

At the beginning of your gardening career try always to manage with fewer rather than more gardening tools. You will gradually find that certain tools are the ones that you use most frequently, even for the 'wrong' tasks. You can add to your armoury at any time, particularly as you take up some specialist task such as the building of a pool or the erection of a wall. It is a waste of time and money to have the shed filled with expensive tools which are never used.

### The Law-nmower

One of the more expensive tools is a lawn-mower. One must make up one's mind what type to buy in the early days, and it is advisable to choose with care and with knowledge, because the expense can be considerable and you cannot normally change your mind once you have made your purchase. Much will depend on the type and size of your garden and the use to which you put your grass. For a very small garden an inexpensive hand-powered machine will suffice. This will have a cylinder cutting-movement, will be light in weight, and will almost certainly run on side wheels. Although it will not be expensive, for very little more it will be possible to buy an electric-powered machine, run via a flex from within the house. This seems to worry some people, who think that the flex will get in one's way and there will be a constant danger of cutting the flex and electrocuting oneself.

Electricity in the garden can be a danger and for this reason the manufacturers of all electric garden tools have gone to extreme lengths to make them safe, even against the most foolish and reckless behaviour. Any woman who can manage an electric vacuum cleaner in the home can manage an electric lawn-mower. These are normally of the type that cut the grass by slashing it with a blade or series of blades which revolve at high speed parallel with the lawn. Some have grass collectors, some do not. All start at the touch of a switch and are blessedly quiet.

Hand- or electric-powered machines are suitable for lawns of up to 100-200 sq yds (say 100-200m²), depending to some extent on the energy of the gardener and the type of lawn. Neither machine will operate satisfactorily on long or wet grass.

For larger gardens or areas of grass one should have a machine powered either by a petrol engine or one with a battery as a power source. Battery mowers have some of the advantages of electric machines (silence and ease of starting) but they are heavy, the batteries must be charged after every use, and regardless of how well they are looked after the batteries do not last as long as the machines and hence must be replaced, a significant addition to the primary cost.

As with all other garden tools, it pays to buy the best machine mower that you can afford, so long as its size is compatible with the area to be mown. Remember that for up to eight months or so of the year you will be using your mower about once a week. So it should be a machine with which you feel comfortable and at ease. It should be easy to start, moderately quiet, light enough to move about the garden, easy to clean, and preferably simple to service. The cost in time and money of having a mower serviced professionally these days is almost prohibitive and you will make an enormous saving if you can carry out such simple tasks as changing the oil and cleaning the air filter and plug, sharpening the blades and oiling the chains. It really is not difficult if you have been provided with a simple manual and a list of spare parts. Get your machine serviced before the grass-cutting season comes round again, preferably at the end of the previous season so that it is put away in a clean and serviceable condition.

Do not buy too large a machine under the misapprehension that this will enable you to get the lawn cut more quickly. Large machines are heavy, unwieldy and awkward in comparison to their smaller brothers and you will find that the lighter and more agile versions allow you to get around the garden much more quickly.

Powered mowers can operate either with the cutting blades fixed around a revolving cylinder or with the blades revolving parallel to the ground. They can have the power operating the propulsion as well as the blades or the blades only. Self-propelled models are usually less tiring, and where necessary it is always possible to use the clutch to disengage the power from the wheels or roller. The best finish for a fine lawn is provided by a machine with a revolving cylinder, propelled by a ribbed or smooth roller at the rear, but a perfectly adequate finish can be obtained from a good rotary cutter, which has a further advantage in that it will attack both long grass and wet grass, whereas a cylinder machine will have difficulty here.

The time and labour involved in mowing a large area of lawn comes mainly from stopping the machine, lifting of the grass box, transporting the contents to some central collecting point, taking the box back to the mower, fixing it in place, and then starting up again. The ideal mower would be one which collected the grass cuttings and instantly either reduced them to a liquid which could spread as fertilizer on to the lawn as the machine moved forward, or reduced them to a fine ash which could again be deposited as movement continued.

As I explained earlier, a good way to reduce the starting and stopping time for the emptying of the grass box is to dot about the garden in convenient positions a number of large plastic or hessian sheets.

A word about laying down lawn mowings. Often we are told by friends who have followed this practice that they are sure that the grass contains many weed seeds because they find that weed plants grow where the mowings have been laid down. On enquiry we find that the merest scattering has been made. In this case the weeds most likely would have grown anyway, and the mowings have been virtually wasted. It is important to make deep mulches, one or two inches (3-5cm) thick at least. No weed seeds will grow up through these. Any seeds which actually germinated will soon die from the heat generated by the grass.

When you drag the mowings away look first for areas where such mulches will be beneficial in more ways than one, for instance alongside a row of peas. When you come to pick these you will walk on the spongy grass mulch instead of panning the soil. When the peas are finished and pulled out, simply rake the mulch aside and on to the used soil and you will find a moist and crumbly area of soil into which a drill for new seed of any kind can be easily drawn right away.

Use these deep mulches also to reserve places in borders where it is intended to plant some shrub or special plant when you buy it. Again, the weeds will be kept at bay and the soil will be moist and in fine condition, as well as having become more enriched and worm aerated in the meantime. All you have to do, if it has not fully disintegrated, is to push it aside, plant and then re-use it as a mulch around the newly established plant.

**Other Powered Tools**

Regardless of how offset the wheels or rollers are on any machine there is still no mower which will cut the grass immediately at the base of a tree or next to a wall or fence. It is possible to buy small auxiliary machines to do this, but in the long run these probably waste more time and energy than a simple walking round with long-handled shears. In some locations it is helpful at the beginning of the season to weedkill the area immediately next to a tree trunk or a wall, so that for the remainder of the summer little or no growth (except perhaps a little moss) will be made in these position. Use a special type of weedkiller called Weedol, for this will kill only green and growing vegetation, will not harm the hard, brown bark of the tree and will not taint the soil in any way. Apply it with care and delicacy and you will be saved much work for the remainder of the year.

New gardeners, particularly men with a leaning towards the mechanical, often wish to use mechanical cultivators in their plots, hoping that by so doing they will dig and prepare the soil both more quickly and more thoroughly than they can do by manual digging. If a large area is involved a machine of this kind can be helpful. When clearing a plot preparatory to sowing grass seed for a fair sized lawn it can sometimes be most helpful to use a rotary cultivator, for this will more or less dig and pulverize in one action. But once the lawn has been made, what other use is there for the expensive and bulky machine? It is unnecessary in all but the largest vegetable gardens.

Instead of buying a cultivator it is much cheaper and more satisfactory in every way to hire one for the few hours or few days that it will be needed to carry out some specific task. It is also possible to buy or hire multi-purpose machines with power-take-off facilities which will run a saw, a cultivator, a hedge clipper, a mower, a pump, a trailer, and the like.

## Chemicals in the Garden

In addition to hand tools and power tools there are also chemical tools: herbicides, insecticides, and fungicides. One chemical weed-killer, for example, has been called a 'chemical hoe' because it carries out so well some of the tasks for which this implement is intended.

Chemicals in the garden are a source of controversy and are responsible for a good deal of disquiet. There are those who will have nothing to do with them, who say that they are poisons, and who try to eat only foods that have not been contaminated by them in any way. But there are also those who say with truth that without insecticides and fungicides the world would starve. The answer for the average small gardener is, I think, that so long as you are aware and responsible, so long as you know what you are doing and what you are using, then all is well. But by the words 'aware' and 'responsible' I mean that you must know what chemical you are using, what are its limitations and its dangers not only to humans but also to all sections of the animal world; you must use it in as limited an application as possible and only as a last resort, and you must use it in the smallest possible quantities with the greatest possible care.

Fortunately the manufacturers and distributors of garden chemicals are intensely aware of the possible dangers of their products to the ecological balance, and it will surprise many critics to see how carefully and thoroughly they are formulated and tested before it is proposed to market them. In many countries even after this there must be official tests, far more stringent than normal conditions of use, before the materials are finally passed for use.

If we go back to our weedkillers we will find that there are three different kinds, with variations within these three. There is the total weedkiller which will kill any green vegetation which it touches yet will not affect brown and woody growth and is completely inactivated when it touches the soil. Then there are the total weedkillers which again kill all vegetation but also poison the soil for some months, sometimes for up to a year, so they can only be used with safety on paths, drives, courtyards, and the like, where they fulfill a most useful purpose. And finally there are the so called selective or hormone weedkillers which are used on grass lawns and which will kill broad leaved plants but will not affect the slender foliage of grass.

All of these have a place in the gardener's shed and all of them can save him a great deal of work and time if he uses them properly. There are various formulations by various manufacturers, so read labels very carefully before you buy and make sure that you have the right product. Make sure also that you use them correctly. Never increase the recommended quantities as this can do real harm. Keep a special watering can for weedkillers and mark this clearly so that it cannot be used for anything else. If you cannot do this, wash out the can with detergent water and several rinses before it is used for anything else.

Weedkillers are intended to kill only weeds, that is, any kind of plant which is growing where it is not wanted. But insecticides cover a somewhat wider range. These, make no mistake about it, are poisons. They are mainly used to clear infestations of aphids, caterpillars, ants, earwigs, slugs, whitefly, red spider mites, and the like, but they can kill such beneficial insects as bees and ladybirds, so they must be used with great care. Some insecticides are made with one specific purpose only, e.g., to kill aphids only. They will have little or no effect on certain other pests. Other insecticides work on a broader spectrum and will kill nearly all garden pests. Some insecticides are what is called systemic, which means that a sprayed plant absorbs the poison into the sap in its system where it stays for some weeks. During the whole of this time any insect piercing a stem or leaf to get at the sap or any insect eating the leaf will receive a dose of the poison. This means that we need not spray so frequently, but it also means that certain food crops can be toxic for some time. So for food crops it is wise to use a non-toxic insecticide or one with a life only of one or two days.

Insecticides usually come in the form of a concentrated liquid or powder. They are normally mixed with water and diluted to be used as a spray. Some powders are used direct from puffer packs. All should be kept in a safe place out of the reach of children and where they cannot suffer accidental damage. Try not to buy in large quantities, for if some portion remains unused it is only too likely that the label will get lost and you will then have to guess what the pack contains, or more wisely you will have to throw it away.

And if you dislike using insecticides in any case, you will find that soapy water from the laundry will often clear your plants of greenfly or caterpillars for a short time.

Fungicides are often trouble preventers rather than cures. If your roses are prone to mildew, then spray them regularly from early summer onwards and you will keep them clean. It is usually possible to mix certain fungicides with insecticides and so do two jobs at once. Some preparations are made in this form and other fungicides are available in systemic formulations.

Gardeners should understand that insecticides and fungicides are necessary to a certain extent because of their own failings. If plants are grown well they will be strong and sturdy enough to withstand attacks by some insects and some diseases, so the aim should always be to grow the best possible plants, not only because you get better value that way, but because it will help you to cut your chemical costs. One should remember, too, that we do not all encourage predators such as birds, toads, frogs, fast moving beetles, and other insects that will help to keep our plants healthy and clean.

One way of attracting birds into your garden is to provide them with a constant supply of water in large, shallow containers from which they can drink and in which they can bathe. It is important that these be kept filled with water at all times so that the birds come to expect it both summer and winter. It will be a convenience here to have an outside water supply so that you do not have to carry jugs of water out from the kitchen and for the serious gardener a convenient water supply is essential. It need be no more than a standpipe on an outside wall of the house, for it is easy enough to lead a hose from here to any part of the garden, but if you have a greenhouse it is probable that you will have water going to this.

**The Garden Frame**
Some of the advantages of running a greenhouse are mentioned in Chapter 2, but so far there has been no discussion about garden

frames, which are, in effect, miniature unheated greenhouses. A frame is a semi-permanent structure of any convenient size with walls not less than about 1ft (30cm) high in the front, sloping upwards to two or three times this height at the back, the whole structure covered with glass in a removable frame. The slope should obviously face south to get greatest warmth from the sun.

The frame gives the protection necessary for young seedlings and there are means of warming it so that it becomes in effect a miniature forcing house. The easiest way today of warming the frame is to install soil warming cables in the soil at the base and, if required, air warming cables on the sides. This form of heating gives gentle and easily controlled warmth at comparatively low cost and it can be allied to a thermostat to keep the temperature at the required level.

Failing an electricity supply it is possible to warm a frame with the old-fashioned but still useful method. Dig out the soil at the base for several inches and fork in no less than, say, 6in (15cm) of fresh farmyard manure, replacing the soil on top of this. The manure will heat up and provide a surprising amount of warmth. If you have no source of fresh farmyard manure, use grass mowings, again fresh, and treat them in exactly the same way. They again will warm the soil above.

Whereas a frame is a fixture, a cloche is portable but serves much the same purpose, that of providing protection to young or tender plants. Cloches are used mainly in the vegetable garden and they help to prolong the growing season by warming the soil and protecting plants in early spring and late autumn. They can be of glass or plastic, the latter material being more frequently seen today simply because of its convenience and low price.

### Paving in the Garden

Another comparatively new product of the greatest value to the gardener because of its convenience and low price is prefabricated, reconstituted stone in the form of paving slabs and walling stone. Units can be as plain as you like or come with various finishes and even colours. They make the laying of paving and the building of walls a simple matter which can be carried out swiftly and with ease by the veriest amateur. By choosing designs and unit sizes carefully (the manufacturers are always willing to advise) it is possible even for those with weak muscles to build an attractive wall which should stand as an attractive and useful garden feature for ever.

Just as paving in a garden need not be only for the patio or terrace, so a garden wall need not be only a boundary wall. Both features can be most useful in the creation of what I call a garden power point, a small area in which are gathered together a shed, with doors wide enough for the passage of a mower, a greenhouse if you want one, compost bins, peat bales, a bonfire point and anything else of a like nature. If you keep everything together you can save yourself much time and frustration. Pave this area completely, for you will wish to use it at all seasons and frequently with heavy loads. Make it compact, yet leave space for bales of peat to be stacked, for cloches to be stored, for boxes of plants to be stood out on a warm spring day. Low walls can make a series of divisions or bays for your different items.

However neat and efficient you make this power point it will never be pretty, so hide it from the rest of the garden by a curtain of shrubs or something as dual purpose as a row of cordon apples or pears. Yet do not site it too far away so that it is inconvenient or hide it so efficiently that one must go through a maze of shrubs to reach it. Remember, too, that whereas the greenhouse should be in full sun, the shed is better in the shade, as are compost bins, peat bales, the cane store, and the water butts.

# 6

## RESTORING A NEGLECTED GARDEN

The turnover of houses today is a fairly rapid process and few places stay empty for long. But there are occasions when through legal delays, or deaths or indecisions in a family, when a property can lie empty for months and even years, and when this happens it is astonishing what a difference can come over what perhaps was once a neat, sophisticated, cultivated garden. The grass will have grown rank and tall and may have brambles and unexpected trees growing in it. There may be holes, sometimes of considerable size, where some animal has made itself at home. One or two trees may have fallen and branches of some will almost certainly lie in the grass. It will be impossible in some parts to define flower beds or borders, or even paths. For some reason and from some place considerable rocks will have appeared and perhaps the odd half brick or two. The pool will be almost indistinguishable from the remainder of the garden, for so many leaves and so much debris will have fallen in that seeds will have germinated in the rich mixture and become first bogland and then dry land. Trees and shrubs will have grown into each other, roses will have developed into long, lank, flowerless stems or may have reverted through suckers to their wild state.

It can be a depressing experience to take over a garden in this state, and the temptation is to put a bulldozer through the lot; or an inexperienced gardener might think in terms of buying a large can or two of weedkiller and getting rid of everything so that a fresh start can be made. Certainly it is a problem where to begin and what to do first to regain control of an area which has gone wild and rampant.

### Where to make a start
A dear friend of mine used to say when faced with a crisis, 'Now let us all be very calm,' and there can be no better advice to give to the gardener with the problem of the neglected plot. The advice I

would add would be to begin with the house and work outwards.

For example, if the garden is totally overgrown you will have problems getting your car in and out, in turning, in transporting your many goods to and fro. So, on the basis that if anything about your garden proves to be irritating or frustrating it must be changed at once, it would seem advisable first of all to clear up those parts of the garden that hinder you in this way. Don't be too thorough at first and take no steps which are irreversible. Cut back vegetation to allow freedom of movement and ease of access, but don't hack it back. If you are in doubt and it is possible, tie it back until it can be identified and then treated correctly. Remove any obstacles. Allow in light and air. Make sure that drains are unblocked, paving secure and buildings safe, particularly doors and windows. Once your car can get in and out easily and delivery or collection vehicles also have simple access, then you can begin to tackle less immediately urgent problems.

Next go carefully around the house walls on the exterior. Check that down pipes are secure and efficient and that drains are clear and can cope with the considerable quantities of water that sometimes flood down in a summer storm. Make sure that the damp proof course of the house is at least 6in (15cm) above the soil surface and if it is not remove the soil to this level. Check that any air bricks or ventilation holes under the house are also clear and working efficiently. Look at all exterior framing to doors and windows to make sure that it is sound and waterproof.

If wall-clinging vines have grown too rampant and are covering windows or concealing possible damage to the roof, clip these back to a safe distance. Do not be in a hurry to wrench these off the surface. Those myriads of leaves may be acting like tiny roof tiles and conducting the rain downwards, keeping the walls dry and secure. Wait until the leaves have fallen from the clipped portion, then you can see any possible damage. Where large vines such as wisteria, trees or shrubs are growing close to the walls of the house, examine the stone or brick work, looking for signs of cracking or subsidence. Make sure that any paving immediately around the house slopes gently away from rather than into the house. Check where underground workings lie, those pipes that supply gas, water, electricity, and where the drains run. Ensure that inspection covers are accessible and moveable and that you can get at mains taps and stopcocks.

Once you have reassured yourself on all these points you will know that however rampant, menacing even, the garden looks, it has not harmed the interior of your home, and you can proceed with a settled mind to the creation of a pleasant and productive plot from the present wilderness.

But being now reassured of the safety and solidity of your property, do not proceed to attack this wilderness with ferocity, but rather extend yourself slowly and gently into its depths. Working gradually outwards from the house, first cut down the grass to manageable heights so that you can see what lies beyond and what may trip you up underfoot. If possible use hand implements at first: hedge clippers or a scythe for larger areas. The use of a machine at this stage is dangerous because it is likely to be damaged on some unseen obstruction, and at the same time it is almost impossible with a machine to avoid cutting down or damaging severely some plant hidden in the grass which you would like to have kept. As you see any plant which is not itself grass fold the grass down around it so that you can either identify it or get some idea of its dimensions. If it is worth keeping, cut the grass short around it and as soon as you can mulch around it with lawn mowings.

Once these discovered plants are allowed light and air again they will develop and reveal their true personalities and you will then be able to decide whether to keep them or not. But it would be a pity to kill or cut down some plant which later could be of service or pleasure simply because of your own haste in clearing the plot.

Cut down the grass only to a manageable height and, if you can, burn it. This suggestion will be unpopular in some quarters, but I give it advisedly because this grass will be rank and full of seeds and goodness knows what else. It will take a considerable time to rot down into good compost and while stacked will be a perfect home for the many slugs that are bound to have collected in this neglected plot.

When you come upon some object other than a plant in the grass, skirt it carefully, clear the grass around it until you have been able to determine with certainty what it is. It might be a piece of brick, the edging to a path which you will be able to follow and to define, a long lost garden tool, a rotting bucket, or it may be the base of a tree or shrub which you cannot identify because of the season. If there is a lawn, once it is defined you can make an enormous difference if you can clear the edges. Even if you think that later you may curve borders which at the moment are straight, trim them as they are. They will be easy enough to change later, and your present voyage is one of discovery. Take a garden line, stretch it taut close to the edge and then trim this edge by pushing in a spade along the line. The spade need not go deep and this method works best if you turn the spade back to front. Having done the trimming, remove the cut pieces of edge, shake off any soil on to the border, and then with the spade or a small border fork gently push the soil away from the lawn edge into the border. You will then be able to trim the grass edges quickly and easily. Immediately the whole scene will look considerably smarter.

Gradually you will find that the original garden begins to take shape. When you reach a certain object and find that it continues in a certain direction, you may have discovered the beginning of a hedge, a row of raspberries, a fence, or a garden frame. You may consider that it is absurd to have this plant or this feature in this spot, but do not attempt immediately to remove it because there was a reason at one time for its location and you are not yet in a state where you can decide on the validity of this reason.

If the garden is a large one this voyage of discovery may take some considerable time, and as you reach out further and further from the house the land that you treated earlier will begin to sprout grass again and weeds will begin to reappear simply because you have improved conditions for them. So you will have to maintain and gradually improve your earlier workings at the same time that you are still extending your frontiers. There is no harm in this other than the fact that it tends to slow down somewhat the overall revealing of the garden plot. The area that you are having to mow once again will improve in appearance each time, and remember that this is the part of the garden nearest to the house, so the improvements you have made will be most noticeable. Meanwhile you will be able to collect useful lawn mowings. Place these around plants on top of the existing grass, but not so close to the plant stems that they themselves may become rotted. The grass and the weeds under this mulch will be the objects of your attention.

This clearance programme and the gradual improvement of the plot may take some months, perhaps even a year or so. During this time many unexpected treasures may come to light if you are patient, snowdrops, daffodils, lilies, and fritillarias perhaps in spring and others as the seasons come and go. So try to be patient and finally when you have gone over the whole plot and revealed the overgrown design made by the previous owner, try not to be in too great a hurry to make changes. Try to live with the plot as you have revealed it for four complete seasons so that you can understand the reason for this tree or the importance of having the pool here and the shed there. You may not agree with the previous owner and you may prefer to make major alterations, but by living with the existing garden your own ideas will come to take shape with reason and sensibility rather than as a mere desire for change and you will find that if you decide to preserve certain features you will be saving yourself both cash and effort. Meanwhile, prune all trees and shrubs of dead wood, burn this, and treat evil weeds such as convolvulus, couch grass, and docks with Weedol.

There is just one important creative step that you can take right at the beginning, when you first start your programme of clearance. If you wish to plant certain new trees and shrubs simply because you love them and have always wanted some specimens of your own, then make yourself a little nursery bed and plant young specimens out in this. Young plants are much less expensive than those which are more mature, and you may be able to take a cutting or layer a specimen in a friends' garden. Then let them grow in your own place rather than in expensive nursery soil or insignificantly in your friend's garden. Look after the plants well, keep them staked and secure. By the time your clearance has been completed and you are gradually changing the garden to suit your own convenience and your own wishes, the young trees or shrubs will have matured considerably and can be moved to their more permanent positions to take up the role that you had assigned to them. You will have saved both time and money, and, equally important, you will have got to know something about these plants, their personalities, their likes and dislikes. Equally, they will have adapted themselves to the soil and to the climate they have discovered in your garden and they will consequently grow more easily and healthily than if they had been newly imported as semi-mature examples.

Another way to cut costs will be with your lawn, for although this may look yellowed, coarse and tussocky at the moment, it can be improved out of all recognition. To dig it up and sow a new lawn will be a very considerable task and a not inconsiderable expense. The grasses may appear to be rough and coarse at this stage of clearance, but constant mowing will help to kill or clear the coarser grasses and encourage those types that have a finer and greener appearance.

Weeds in the grass can be cleared easily enought by the application of hormone weedkillers of a feed-and-weed granular mixture. It may take a year or two but you will find that the rough grass gradually becomes a lawn with no expense other than the routine weekly mowing. Our own large expanse of lawn has been made simply by mowing paddock and orchard grass.

## Problems with Trees

You will probably find that although you disagree with some of the planning and some of the features that have been revealed, it may be necessary to retain some simply because the disruption caused by removing them would be greater than the possible benefit. This is particularly the case with existing trees. You may find that one large and overgrown tree gives too much shade on one portion of the ground, or perhaps it blocks an attractive view. But to take down this vast tree and to grub out its roots would be a task completely beyond you with your own available tools and labour and beyond you financially if you use skilled imported labour.

Look at this problem tree carefully and try to decide whether some judicious pruning and clearing could make a difference. If you have no experience of working with trees do not attempt to do the work yourself unless you can do it under supervision and tuition. You will probably find that a reputable tree surgeon will be able to improve the shape or thickness of the tree in a single day. Never, never climb the tree and saw off pieces from a number of branches under the impression that these branches will make new but less dense growth, and leave the poor tree amputated, naked with hat-peg like extremities. This way can lead only to a badly shaped and unsatisfactory tree for the remainder of its life and could indeed kill it.

If the tree needs thinning, try to select certain main branches which can be removed completely to allow in light and air. Then, if you are doing it yourself, cut first the thin, spindly outer extremities of the branch, working gradually inwards towards the main trunk. This way you will lighten the weight of the branch so that when you finally sever it at the point where it joins the main trunk you can do this to make a clean wound which will heal quickly and thoroughly. If you try to cut out the branch completely at one time it will be almost impossible to prevent damage and tearing to the fabric of the tree. You may also damage plants growing below because you will not be able to control the fall of the heavy branch.

In the same way it is possible to take out and remove the whole of the top or the crown of the tree, and so to reduce its size and make it more suitable for its site. But as I have said before, do not attempt any of this unless you have had experience or can be guided by someone who knows what he is doing.

Whenever any amputation has been made on a tree or shrub, make sure that this goes back to a main trunk or branch. Pare the wound with a sharp knife to trim off all ragged or torn edges and leave a good, clean, smooth area of bare wood. Then treat this with a proper preservative such as Arbrex, covering the wound completely to keep out disease spores and rain. Every wound more than about 2in (5cm) in diameter should be treated in this way. The outer skin or cambium layer of the tree will gradually grow over the edges of the wound to protect it from the elements and to hide or disguise the scar.

Working with trees like this can be a lengthy, difficult, and even dangerous business. One frequent cause of damage to persons or property is a failure to remove away from the site the debris that has been brought down from the tree. When a branch is gradually cut down the twigs will lie first on the ground, occupying considerable space, and will be followed by larger pieces of the branch and finally by the heavier portions of the bough as the main trunk is reached. If all this is permitted to lie where it falls it can easily trip one up, and when this happens with a saw in the hand a nasty cut can be the result. So at regular intervals it is well worth while removing all the debris collected and either burning it or keeping it in some safer place to be dealt with later. Small twigs can be kept in plastic bags and used as kindling for a fire and the larger pieces cut into convenient lengths for stacking and drying.

To remove an entire tree can be a very considerable operation, particularly where space is confined, as in a small town garden surrounded by buildings. But wherever the task is to be undertaken, never, ever, except where there is plenty of space to spare and where you have had previous experience, try to emulate the traditional lumberjack and cut through the base of the tree to send it crashing with the bellowed warning, 'Timber!'

Once again take it slowly, piece by piece, working inwards towards the trunk and clearing as you go. Make up your mind from the beginning whether you are going to cut the tree down more or less to ground level and leave the roots or whether you are going to dig them out too and have finished with the problem completely. Dependant on your decision on this matter will be the means you adopt, for if you choose to grub out the tree roots rather than have them in your way in the garden for a matter possibly of years, then you will be advised to leave the lower 10ft (3m) or so of trunk, clearing away every bough and branch so that the trunk stands naked and unobstructed. This trunk will be a tremendous help in exerting leverage on the thick and tenacious roots which so often spread so far underground.

So when you have taken off all the side branches and are left only with the main trunk, first dig a channel around the base of the tree near to the trunk and extending outwards for up to 3ft (1m) or so. As you meet main roots cut them and where necessary cut out any portion of them that obstructs your digging. Every now and again try to rock the tree on its roots by means of the leverage from the trunk. It will help to tie a stout rope or two to the top of this trunk which you can get several people to pull on and let go so that the tree gradually rocks more and more. You will find that this rocking process loosens the soil and reveals more roots to be cut. Gradually the rocking will become more and more pronounced until finally the trunk will fall to the ground, ripping out by itself its few remaining roots. It can then be cut into portions and taken away, while the hole excavated can be filled, returfed and the garden restored to order.

If the tree is in a position where any stump remaining can be easily concealed, or where the land is spacious enough to warrant leaving it, then you are saved all the laborious business of digging out the roots. In this case you can either saw down the tree as near as possible to ground level or you can leave a stump possibly as a base for a seat or a table, a bird bath or similar feature, or as the prop on which you can grow a climbing clematis, a rose or a decorative ivy.

If the tree is not dead you will be wise to kill it in case it sends out new growth. Do this by boring into the trunk a number of holes an inch or more in diameter and at least 6in (15cm) deep. Fill these with a 50/50 mixture of old engine oil and brushwood killer and let this soak in. You will find that you can do this once a week or so for some months, but the damage will have been done in the first month or two. Suckers will die and all growth will be killed. Gradually, very gradually, the stump and the roots will begin to rot away and in course of time, depending on the type of tree, it will all disappear.

If there is safe space and you are not prepared to wait what could be a matter of some years, and if it will not be a nuisance to the neighbours, at the end of the first year build a large bonfire over the stump, get it going well and then damp it down with moist weeds or something of that nature so that the fire will last some time but will not blaze too fiercely or dangerously. The stump will slowly begin to smoulder, even underground. Take care that other trees or plants you treasure are not too close, otherwise it is possible that they might be damaged.

There are a few trees which are actively dangerous near a house or wall, especially when the soil is of a heavy clay. The roots stretch out and are greedy for water. Abstracting this from the soil causes shrinkage and cracking, and wall foundations are apt to sink. Roots will also penetrate drainage pipes and crack or break these. So never allow a poplar, for example, nearer than 100ft (say 30m) from a house and in general try to make a rule that no large tree grows nearer than 20ft (6m). This may be carrying safety a little too far, but bills for restoring subsidence or cracked foundations can be very high. I am aware in saying this that some critics will point to the rows of poplar trees growing along the sides of so many French roads, one of the glories of that magnificent country, and say that the foundations of these roads have not been damaged by the tree roots; and to this I would agree with some qualifications, for road surfaces are not always what they should be; and their deficiencies are often attributable to root damage. A further reply could also be that the camber of these roads sends towards the boundary trees just about every drop of water that might fall, so that they obtain their satisfaction from this.

### Shrubs and Hedges

Most shrubs and climbers which actually grow on house walls have root systems which can provide sufficient nourishment for the remainder of the plant from the least possible amount of moisture. The soil immediately next to the house or any building walls is always dry, partly because it is sheltered from rains by the actual structure and partly because much of the soil moisture is absorbed by the brick, stone or concrete of the wall on which it is growing. Try to remember this fact when planting any new climber and make sure that in its first weeks it receives the moisture that it requires and which in its more mature stages it can often find from the air as well as from the soil.

Shrubs growing elsewhere in the garden are generally easier to prune to size and shape than a tree, because they are in essence somewhat smaller and more spreading in outline. Where there must be drastic reduction in size, cut out whole branches down to the ground or to a main stem rather than trying to clip the shrub as you might a hedge. If drastic pruning appears necessary, do this by degrees, half of it spread over one year and the other half over the next, to avoid too great a shock to the shrub's system. Where you find rampant wild shrubs such as dog roses and prickly brambles, take it easily, work from the nearest tip of a branch and cut off sections. These will be easier to load on to a barrow or sheet and take away to burn. When finally you reach the crown of the plant it can more easily be dug out or killed.

Hedges in a neglected garden are nearly always overgrown to the extent that they hang over paths, interfere with the growth of other plants, and give the place an untidy and unrecognizable appearance. There is no means of knowing whether herbaceous plants are growing underneath them. Nearly all hedging material can be cut back severely in late winter, right into the old wood, but always do one side at a time. The hedge will look awful, brown, bare, and thin, but new growth will soon appear. Let this become established so that it promotes the health of the plants for a year before tackling the other side of the hedge. Remember, too, that hedges are plants and need food and moisture at the roots just as much as the other plants in the garden. Give them a long lasting feed of a handful of bonemeal to every 1yd (1m) of hedge and follow this if you can with a good mulch of moist peat or compost.

Try always to trim the top of your hedges so that they are slightly narrower than the base. This way they will allow greater fall of rain into the hedge and its base and will suffer less damage and breaking in the event of heavy snowfall. If you wish to maintain geometrically straight lines for your hedge, do not rely on your eye alone when trimming it. Insert a stout post or a length of angle iron at the necessary intervals along the hedge depending on its length and stretch heavy gauge galvanized wire between them at the height you have chosen. Work to this level. The wire should not show, of course, nor should the posts and they will not do so if they are set back from the surface of the hedge and if the trimming is carried out correctly.

Hedges are often a trap for miscellaneous leaves, pieces of paper or plastic, and other debris which gets blown up against the barrier in periods of strong winds. Much of this will rot down and do little but good, but some items such as the pieces of plastic can last for years before degenerating, and if the hedge is anywhere near a public highway it is almost certain to recieve its quota of discarded cigarette packets and cans. So once a year or so go along the length of any hedges and clear out any materials that will not be conducive to its health, growth, and good looks.

## Other Problems

But hedges are not the only places in old and neglected gardens where debris is likely to be found. Depending on the area and the age of the premises, some place in the garden will be found to be built almost entirely on a pile of rotting tins, pram wheels, buckets and kettles, sauce and beer bottles, and the like. There can be whole mounds of rubbish of this nature, or you may trace it through the crunch of your spade as you dig what might appear to be virgin soil. Needless to say all this debris should be removed so far as is possible. But a word of advice: go carefully. It is possible that you might stumble upon some discard which because of its age or its scarcity now has some modest commercial value. Old bottles in particular can be picked up in good condition and once they have been cleaned they can often be sold to a local junk shop for a worthwhile sum. The remainder of the debris is not worth saving and is of no value even as rubble for foundations or for a soakaway, for it is either already in a state of semi-disintegration or will shortly reach that stage. If your local rubbish disposal service will not accept large quantities of debris like this, telephone your town hall to find out the location of a local tip where you can take it loaded into plastic sacks.

Fencing posts, pergolas, and other timber structures may be found to be rotting and in a dangerous state. It will usually be found that to try to repair these is a mere waste of time. As fences and pergolas are semi-permanent structures, it is advisable to renew them in the neglected garden only if you are certain you will enjoy the features that they outline. If you are still clearing and still investigating and come across irreparably damaged items such as these, it is wiser to remove them and leave the site vacant to be used later according to the plans that will be gradually maturing in your mind as the clearance programme progresses.

Timber is relatively expensive today, so it is well to make the most of it. Always treat with a copper-based preservative any timber part that you use in the garden. Any part that will go under or have contact with the soil can be heavily painted with creosote, but use this material with care, for its fumes are strong enough to kill or severely damage plants for a long time after the first treatment. Never try to grow climbers on a newly creosoted fence, for example, but use instead one of the proprietary substances specially made for this purpose which are normally available in several colours.

The neglected garden was once a product of a person's mind, muscle, and horticultural skill and as such it should not be dismissed out of hand once the preliminary clearance has been completed. But on the other hand the art or science of gardening is in a way an expression of one's own personality on the land and the materials growing in that land. So too slavish a following of previous layouts would be a surrender of your own creative skills and a failure to express fully your own thoughts and feelings in the garden. Never dismiss too quickly what someone has done before, because there was a reason for it. But that reason may have disappeared with the advent of more modern materials or with newer varieties of plants. Try to make a garden of the future rather than one of the past. Accept what you find to be good, build what you know will be needed, and create what you wish to see and enjoy in the future, always remembering that as the years pass you will wish to engage a little less in the more vigorous and taxing aspects of gardening. So create a layout or a system that will allow for a tapering off of demands on energy, while still providing satisfaction and producing food and flowers for your pleasure.

# 7

## STARTING WITH AN EMPTY PLOT

Nothing gives a gardener greater opportunity than having an empty plot with which he can do as he likes. There is nothing to undo, no creations of previous minds to understand, no buildings to raze, no trees to cut down, no fences to replace, no lawn to encourage. Everything can be begun from the beginning. He can dream, visualize, hope; but he has to work, because unfortunately few plots *are* empty.

Once the bare soil outside the house is examined carefully it will usually be found to be littered with half bricks and pieces of stone, with lumps of concrete and baulks of timber, with charred or oily places where there has been a bonfire or a spillage of oil. Sometimes parts of the soil will be virgin and virile topsoil, but too often it will be sour, yellow subsoil which will be lumpy with clay, sticky and heavy to the touch. There may be the odd patch of nettles and brambles, a few dandelions and a patch or two of dispirited couch grass, all struggling hard against their environment but giving an indication that under present circumstances only the strongest and most tenacious of plants can hope to survive.

In such cases obviously the rubbish must be removed, the soil must be brought into good heart, and a plan must be made for the overall treatment of the plot. Accept as philosophically as you can that treatment is going to take some time. It is just no good trying to sow lawn seed or plant herbaceous material in a soil which is sour and sick. Something will eventually grow, but it will be a poor crop and expensive.

### Shrubs and Trees
Once again it will be profitable to make immediate plantings of shrubs and trees so that they may be allowed to grow in your soil and at your expense rather than in the expensive soil of the nursery-

men. Buy small, cheap, immature trees and shrubs, plant them well in a cleared and treated piece of soil and keep this always clear of weeds. In one or two years when you are ready for them they will be larger, stronger, accustomed to your soil and your climate and ready to do justice to your perspicacity and wisdom.

It might be possible in some circumstances to plant one or two trees or shrubs in their permanent positions if you are quite sure of where they are to go and how large they are likely to grow. Whether you plant in a nursery bed or in the final location, your trees and shrubs are an investment and you should take every care of them. A rabbit can rob you of your entire planting in a single night, so surround them with wire netting if this is a possibility. A drying wind or a hot sun can draw more moisture from the plants than the immature roots can replace from the soil, and the plants will die. So spray them nightly if the weather is against them. A strong wind can snap the slender stem of a young tree, so stake it well. Slugs or snails can feed avidly on its tender young foliage, so put down a slug pellet or two under a stone at the base of its stem.

If you make a nursery bed for your young plants see that it will grow them well. Choose a site that will be useful later, for vegetables perhaps or for a rose bed. Dig the area thoroughly and clear away all weeds and debris. Incorporate into the soil some good humus-making material such as farmyard manure, compost, or peat and add a good handful of a balanced fertilizer to every 1 sq yd (1m²) of the plot. Break up the soil so that it is fine and crumbly in texture.

## Making a Lawn

Once you have taken care of the future by planting your young trees and shrubs you can turn your attention to the present and make your plot a more pleasant place to look at. Probably the best way to do this in a short time is to grass it down completely. Do not worry about the location of the various features you wish to construct but put the entire garden down to grass so that it is levelled and furnished. Grass can always be removed and need never be wasted.

First clear all debris and stones from the surface and then, if you enjoy the exercise, start to dig. Dig the entire plot, not too deeply, breaking up the soil as you go and removing all weeds and stones you come across. Incorporate into the soil as much humus-making material as you can obtain or afford. As you dig, it will be possible to roughly level the surface and get rid of major bumps and hollows.

If you do not enjoy or cannot undertake the sometimes heavy labour of large-scale digging, then this is one of the few times when it will be helpful to hire a mechanical cultivator to do the work for you. You will usually find that you can hire by the day or by the week and these machines are usually in good condition. Make sure that you do not take a machine that is too big or too heavy for you; they can be difficult to control or hard to start. Some models are small enough and light enough for almost all women. For a task such as this it will be best to use a machine with rotating blades to chew up and pulverize the soil rather than a straightforward plough type. Do not attempt to go too deeply, for it is not necessary. Spread your humus-making material on top of the soil and dig it in with your machine. You should get a better finish with a machine than with hand digging, but bear in mind the fact that you have not been able to clear away the weeds as you go. Some will die simply because they have been uprooted and slashed, but some others may even be multiplied by the treatment they have received. Every little piece of dandelion root or couch grass stolon is a potential plant.

So once the entire surface has been dug with your machine, go over the area with a rake, smoothing and levelling it and drawing to the surface all the pieces of vegetation that have been chopped by the blades. Collect all this material and burn it rather than attempting to compost it.

The actual process of sowing lawn seed or laying turf has been discussed in Chapter 4 and need not concern us here again, but the grass will take some time to grow through and make a good working surface, so in the meantime it might be well to spend time creatively looking at your boundaries.

**Hedges and Fences**
On most housing estates a new house will have its garden defined only by a post and wire fence. This is unpleasant to look at, incapable of keeping animals or people in or out, useless as a windbreak and serves only to mark the legal confines of the plot. So this post and wire fence should be replaced with something more efficient and pleasant as soon as it is convenient.

The possibilities are several. You can have a brick wall, a stone wall, or one of the openwork precast slabs. You can have a timber fence. You can have a netting fence; galvanized, plastic-covered wire or plastic alone. Any of these can support or help to support a wide range of plants. You can have a hedge. Or you can have a combination of any or all of these. It seems a pity to stick to one uniform type of surround when so often one material is particularly suited to one section and another to another. For example, it might be pleasant to have a solid brick wall beside the area where you plan to build your patio or terrace, for this would both give complete privacy and would serve as a windbreak and a suntrap. This might change into a fence a little further down the garden, while a hedge at the bottom might provide a pleasant green foil for the garden plants, or it may be so situated that you can have a flowering hedge, perhaps of ornamental quince, roses, or hebe. There is no limit to what you can do, and the questions you ask yourself will merely be which materials will be most attractive and most efficient, and what you can afford. Ask yourself too, if you live near a busy road, which materials are most likely to help shut out traffic noise. Incidentally, tall, graceful bamboos are surprisingly good for this purpose, although they take up more space than most of us can normally afford.

When making a decision bear in mind also the facts that some barriers may take a long time to erect, some may involve considerable labour, some may have a limited life, some may not keep out the neighbour's cat, some may block out too much light, some may require constant attention in the way of clipping or shaping, some may absorb too much moisture or food from the soil and so preclude the growth of herbaceous plants nearby. All these points, and possibly others dictated by personal needs or tastes, should be taken into account before a decision is reached. The boundaries of a garden are both important and more or less permanent, for just as their installation means considerable work and expense, so does their demolition or alteration, making it wise to choose correctly in the first place.

It is not the purpose of this book to advise on carpentry or bricklaying, but rather on gardening, and I therefore leave to others more qualified than I to tell how to erect a fence or build a wall, while I concentrate on the horticultural and say a few words about hedges.

There are a number of plants which make good hedges and there are good reasons why some of these are the most frequently seen. There are also a number of plants sometimes recommended for hedging which will, indeed, make an excellent and attractive boundary for a while but which eventually raise more problems and involve more work than they solve or save and which cannot therefore be recommended here, as we are looking for ways of making our gardening easier and therefore more pleasurable. Beware, for instance, of hedge plants which grow too quickly, for they are also likely to grow too large and will soon be out of control. Gardeners today are not so fond of internal hedges as once they were, preferring to divide one section of the garden from another by means of less formal plantings such as a row of dwarf roses, lavender, or santolina, the possible exception being in and near the fruit and vegetable garden, where a hedge or barrier can well be made of cordon fruits, a row of raspberries, or a line of currant bushes.

## Choosing hedging plants

Exterior or boundary hedges must depend upon the size of the garden as well as its main purpose. For some gardens in some localities a rhododendron hedge will look quite natural and will do a first-class job, but for others such a hedge might fill the entire garden! Yet by careful selection it might be possible to choose dwarf evergreen kinds of rhododendron that would fill the requirements. For some it might be well to plant a sophisticated box or yew boundary to be trained and clipped into meticulous shape, while for others only a hawthorn, berberis, or myrobalan plum will be strong and prickly enough to deter farm animals from trespassing.

I cannot myself see much sense in planting a hedge of deciduous materials, for who wants to look at what in effect is a bare wall for several months of the year? But the excellent *Fagus sylvatica*, the common beech, although classed as deciduous, holds its foliage throughout the winter, brown, glossy and rustling in the wind. My prejudices lead me to restrict the following list of hedging plants to whose which are evergreen or which continue to look attractive in the winter months.

*Aucuba japonica* and its varieties will make a good hedge up to about 6ft (2m) high. It is hardy, suitable for sun or shade, and bearing red, yellow, or white berries according to variety, provided male and female plants are close together. Plant 2ft apart (60cm); clip or prune in spring.

Evergreen types of berberis, such as *B. darwinii* and *B. stenophylla* will make colourful hedges, well-flowered in spring, well berried in winter, with attractive leaves, but look out for the wicked thorns. Plant about 2ft apart (60cm) and trim when the flowers have faded.

Box is a fine old hedging material which, for hundreds of years has been used for topiary in this country, which suggests correctly that it stands up well to close clipping. Although very slow to grow, it will live for ever and makes a fine, dense, impenetrable barrier. Plant 2ft apart (60cm) and trim in summer. There is a golden form and a dwarf variety.

Escallonia can make a first-class hedge, attractive, colourful, neat, even standing up to seaside winds, but because the flowers are so pretty, do not let the growth get out of hand. Cut back lightly in spring and once again after the flowers have dropped. There are several cultivars with vivid colour or a tall habit of growth.

A rather less common type of hedging is provided by *Euonymus japonicus*, with dark green shiny foliage. There is a variety with a golden edge to the leaves. Don't use this plant for hedging if your locality is cold and bleak, but otherwise it does well, even by the coast and in cities. Plant 1-2ft apart (30-60cm) and clip in summer.

I have mentioned that the beech is deciduous but still a good hedger. Plant 1-2ft apart (30-60cm) and leave the young plants alone for the first couple of years and then just tip the extreme growth to keep the base of the hedge thick. When it has reached its required height, trim it annually in August. There is a purple form which can be mixed with the green or grown separately.

An ilex or holly hedge is said to be very slow growing, but this has not invariably been my own experience. I would certainly recommend it for its appearance, its hardiness, its efficiency, and its ease of handling. Plant both sexes if you want berries, and don't forget there are gold and silver forms. Plant 1-2ft apart (30-60cm) and prune lightly in late spring for the first few years.

Privet is justly popular as a hedging material in urban districts, for it is neat, thick, easy to cultivate, and tolerant of almost any conditions, even city dust and smoke. But it is a greedy plant and nothing will grow under it unless heavily fed. The golden form is perhaps even more attractive, but this tends to dominate all other colours in the garden. Plant about 1ft apart (30cm) and cut right back to within a foot or so (30cm) at the end of the first winter. Let it grow gradually, keeping it dense by frequent clipping.

Another hedging plant requiring discipline to show at its best is the Chinese honeysuckle, *Lonicera nitida*, a shrubby rather than climbing plant. The small leaves give a neat and attractive appearance. Plant 1ft apart (30cm) and cut back almost at once, maintaining a programme of close clipping to help keep the hedge tight, close, and impenetrable.

So many of our garden trees are members of the prunus family and the same is true of hedging material. Some varieties are deciduous, but these are generally grown as a part of a mixed hedge, where their undoubted qualities can be taken advantage of and their drawbacks disguised. There are today some flowering varieties with purple leaves, like miniature *Prunus pissardi*. You need to see these at a nursery to judge which you would like best. Evergreen types include *Prunus laurocerasus*, the laurel with heavy, thick, green leaves, and *P. lusitanica*, the Portugal laurel, both greedy of space. Plant all of these about 2ft apart (60cm), trim the first in late summer and the evergreen varieties a little earlier.

Some varieties of pyracantha make good hedges and of course the white flowers followed by the red, yellow, or orange berries are an added bonus. Don't trim this plant too closely in the late spring or you will be getting rid of most of your flowers and berries. Plant about 2ft (60cm) apart.

Although I am a great believer in conifers for the garden, evergreen grey, gold, blue, I find them a little dense and heavy as hedging materials except in relatively short lengths for special purposes. *Chamaecyparis lawsoniana*, or Lawson's cypress, makes a first class hedge, thick, quick growing, easy, and tolerant of soils and shade. There are several forms. Plant 1-5ft apart (30-150cm), depending on the height you wish them to attain and trim them only lightly for the first year or two.

Equally good, or perhaps even better for a taller screen, is *Cupressocyparis leylandii*, Leyland's cypress, which really is a fast grower, is quite hardy, and stands up well to clipping. Treat like a Lawson's.

*Taxus baccata*, or yew, is a slow-growing, long-lived plant, seen in so many country churchyards and used for so many topiary pieces. There is a golden form, if the dark green of the common yew seems oppressive and funeral. It is poisonous to cattle, so do not plant where it can be reached by them. Plant about 2ft apart (60cm) and trim once a year in August unless you are cutting to a special shape, in which case more frequent attention will be found to be helpful.

Two final conifers, *Cupressus macrocarpa* and *Thuja occidentalis* present problems. The cupressus has a disconcerting and infuriating habit of dying at the base of the tree if the winter is cold. The golden form, *C. m. lutea*, appears to be rather tougher and so far as I am concerned is also more attractive to look at. The thujas make good hedges only when they are growing on good soil, deep, moist, but well drained, and for this reason they can sometimes put in unsatisfactory performances.

There is no reason why a hedge should be of one type of plant only; it can be as mixed as you like, and the mixtures can vary from a farm hedge type of just about everything rough and serviceable to the sophisticated hedges to be seen at Hidcote Manor garden, where a scarlet *Tropaelum speciosum* trails its way through a solemn dark yew hedge at one point and where at another the hedge is composed of beech, box, holly, hornbeam, and yew all together. But it takes a little courage as well as a certain skill to make one of these 'tapestry hedges.'

Because a hedge is a long-lived structure in the garden it is worthwhile and time and labour-saving in the long run to install it properly. It is easy to estimate the number of plants you will need, and it is always wise to order up to half-a-dozen extra in case there are any failures. Plant the extra ones almost anywhere nearby in the garden and they will then be of the right height and size if you need them at any time.

Mark out the line of the hedge and dig out a trench at least 1ft wide and 1ft deep (30cm x 30cm). Break up the soil at the bottom of the trench and fork in some farmyard manure or some peat, together with some 4oz. (100g) of a proprietary balanced fertilizer to every 1yd (1m) of the trench. Your plants will probably be about 2ft (60cm) tall when you get them. Put them into the trench at the correct intervals, making sure that the soil level finishes up at the existing soil marks on the stems, that the soil level is well trodden down around them, and that they are secure and upright. If you wish to give added support, or if you wish to ensure a good, straight, level line for the top and sides of the hedge, you can, as suggested earlier, erect posts at each end and supports in the centre where necessary and strain heavy gauge galvanized wires between them so they will be hidden by the foliage as the little trees grow. This is better done at the time of planting rather than later.

Keep a close eye on your newly planted hedge for the first few months, making sure particularly that the roots are kept moist when the weather is dry. Try to keep weeds down at the feet of the plants. A good mulch of moist peat or home-made compost will help both to conserve moisture and to keep down weeds, and it will be a labour-saving operation to apply this annually in the spring.

If you are growing a hedge with large leaves, such as a laurel, normal trimming with shears or electric hedge cutters will inevitably cut some of the leaves in half, and this wound will turn brown. This disfigurement can be avoided if you can go to the trouble of pruning rather than clipping, that is, cutting stems rather than leaves.

Rose hedges of old-fashioned and moss roses are sometimes recommended by romantics, and in places like public parks and nurseries they can look most attractive. But they have to be trained and shaped, and weeds have to be cleared from underneath them. After a couple of hours crawling about under a rose hedge, scratched, torn, dirty, and stinging, you will decide that gardening is not the pleasure you once thought it to be. Shrub or old-fashioned roses usually flower and are in leaf for only comparatively brief periods, and modern types do not spread in the same way and so leave gaps at the base. The latter are best for internal divisions, where they can provide scents and colours and give you blooms to pick.

Gaps at the base will also appear even with such splendid material as Chinese honeysuckle and privet if the bushes have been allowed to grow too tall before being cut back. With almost all hedging material it is essential to keep the top cut back in order to encourage growth lower down. If a hedge has been neglected and has grown too wide and straggly, do not attempt to cut it back to size and shape all at once, but do one side one year and the other side the next.

### Growing plants from seed

So by now our empty plot has had some trees and shrubs planted, either in a nursery bed or in their permanent positions; a lawn has been sown and boundary hedges installed. What comes next? Probably a visit to the bank manager, for all this has been expensive, and it is time to draw in the horns and go slow for a while. I suggest there are two simple and effective means to economize at this stage. The first is to raise some plants from seed, from division, from cuttings, and by layering; and the second is to begin growing some vegetables for consumption in the home. As some of the techniques for the second will be explained in describing the first, let us now have a look at the simple methods available to us for raising plants or increasing our stock of them.

After raising many plants from seed it still gives me a thrill, because it seems impossible that these tiny, dried husks, these pellets or this stuff almost like powder can develop into plants a thousand times larger, with a complete circulatory system, all in a matter of a few weeks or a few months. Again, all my life I have said that seeds are too cheap, that they give better value than almost anything else under the sun, and although prices have climbed steeply in recent times they still give wonderful value for the money. Surely nothing else can give returns of at least several hundred per cent in less than a single year!

Seeds are normally sown in a pot or box in a greenhouse or some other sheltered spot, and most seed packets or catalogues will be found to carry printed instructions for successful sowing. Some seeds need quite high temperatures to ensure their germination, and where this is the case it is wise not to attempt to grow them unless you have a greenhouse or a special propagating case. But for most seeds that need not so much high temperatures as merely a modest degree of protection and warmth to bring them into life, then you can make use of a window in your home to act as your greenhouse.

You will need some pots or boxes, some seed compost, and some transparent plastic bags. The idea is to sow the seed very thinly on the surface of the soil in the pot, cover it lightly with more soil, and then pop the pot into a plastic bag. Blow into the bag to inflate it and then seal the mouth with a rubber band or some other method. The pot inside its miniature greenhouse can then be stood on a warm window sill or even placed in a warmer spot such as a heated clothes cupboard. In the latter case the pot *must* be brought out into the light immediately germination takes place. When the seeds begin to form true leaves instead of the one or two cotyledons or seed leaves, the plastic bag is gradually opened to allow the young plants to become accustomed to the outside air, and when they are large and strong enough they can be planted out into individual containers or spaced in rows in boxes, and hardened by being stood outside on good days until the frosts are over, to make good, strong growth before being placed in the soil.

It is important to use a good soil, specially prepared for the task of raising seeds. You can buy in small quantities a mixture known as the John Innes Seed Composts, a balanced blend of soil, peat, sand, and fertilizers which was devised by scientists at the John Innes Horticultural Institution some years ago, or one of the soil-less composts such as Levington and Kerimure. All of these are sterile, which is to say that they have been treated so that they contain no weed seeds, disease spores, or insects. This means that when you see some growth above the soil it can only be the seeds you have sown and not something that was lying dormant in the soil.

When you come to sow seeds out of doors you will notice that your soil is nothing like so fine or even as the John Innes compost or the soil-less mixture, so you must get down to it and break it up until it is fine enough to accept the tiny seeds you wish to put into it. Digging, raking, treading will all help, but you must be patient and appreciate that to drop your tender and tiny seed into a lumpy and stony soil will merely waste it. Make sure too that the soil is moist, not wet but just gently moist.

The usual method of sowing most seed, especially vegetable seed, is in a row. This is a matter of convenience and order, for you will then have your plants readily placed for cultivation instead of being scattered about and in the way. Always try to use a garden line so that you get nice, straight rows. Beside the line make a drill with a hoe or even a pointed stick, just drawing it lightly along the soil to make a narrow channel, often no more than about a $\frac{1}{4}$in deep (5mm) for certain seeds. A general rule is that the drill should be twice the depth of the seed. Sow the seed in this channel as thinly as you can manage and then cover it again with the soil from the side. Tread the soil lightly to firm it down. This will mean that you have hidden the seeds, so never forget to label the row, preferably at both ends, so that you know something is growing there and you know also what it is and when you sowed it.

In the flower border you will not wish to grow plants in straight rows like this but in a more random pattern. One pretty way is to press the rim of a large flower pot into the soil, which will make a circle into which you can place your seeds. But you may not wish to use lines, shapes, or patterns at all, and there is nothing to stop you just scattering your seeds on the soil and covering them with a light sprinkling of more soil. The only trouble here is that when the seeds germinate it may take you a little while before you can identify them as the plant you want or a plant you do not want, a weed.

When the seeds germinate they first send out a pair of leaves known as cotyledons or seed leaves. They were present in the seed and their job is to supply nourishment until the seedling can develop roots and true leaves to take over. Seed leaves are much the same in all seedlings and are of little value in identifying the plant. You have to wait until the next leaves appear, the true leaves, and these bear the characteristic appearance of the plant you have sown. Never try to thin out any plants until their true leaves have appeared, for until this happens they are just too young and weak to take it.

Seeds sown in a row, however thinly you have tried to sow them, will almost certainly have to be thinned once they have germinated and developed their true leaves. It is not wise to let them stay close too long, because then they become drawn and mature, i.e., run to flower, too quickly and then become spent. Flower seed packets are usually explicit about which kinds should be sown where they are to flower, and this usually means that these are kinds which do not transplant well, annual poppies for example, because of the type of tap root they grow. Many others can be carefully thinned out. This might mean prising up a little clump of several so as to let the largest one in the crowd stay in place. The removed seedlings of this sort can then be separated and planted individually, each with 2-3in (5-8cm) to itself, or more space if you know that these are meant to grow into large plants. The less crowded flowering annuals are, the longer they will bloom so long as you keep the faded flowers picked off to prevent them running to seed.

If you find that the site where you hoped to grow the thinnings is not ready, simply find a little patch of good soil and plant them about 3in (8cm) apart each way, and then move them again as soon as they touch. By this time they should have developed a good mass of roots. Always protect roots and never let the plants lie around waiting to be put into the soil with their roots exposed to the sun and air.

### Division, Layering and Cuttings

But there are other means of growing new plants besides sowing seed. Many perennial herbaceous plants, for example, grow into large clumps, and after three or four years their flowers suffer because the plants are being choked. The thing to do here is to dig up the clump and separate or divide the outer portions, which are stronger, into a number of smaller clumps, each of which can be planted wherever you like to widen and increase your enjoyment. This is one means, known as division, of increasing your stock of plants with little or no effort and certainly at no cost.

Another simple method of increasing your stock of plants is by layering, usually applied to low-growing shrubs and occasionally trees. The thing to do here is to take one of the lower branches and bend it down so that some part of it touches the soil. Wound the branch at this point by cutting a little nick in it or by bending it so that the tissue is ruptured but not broken. Treat the nick with hormone rooting powder if you wish, bury the wound very slightly into the soil and hold down the branch by placing a heavy stone on it at this point, or pegging it down with a twig. In time roots will begin to grow at the point of the wound and you can then (usually the following spring) cut the young plant loose from its parent.

Taking cuttings is still another way of increasing your stock at little or no cost, but we enter here a rather wider and more complex world, for there are stem cuttings, leaf cuttings, and root cuttings, and the stem cuttings can be hard, soft, or half-ripe; so I propose not to complicate matters by going into detail. The idea, briefly, is that a growing portion of a plant is separated from that plant and treated in one of several ways to create a new plant.

There is everything to be said for propagating your own plants, except that it will save time; for it will not. It will cost time but save much money and if this statement wreaths the young reader's face in smiles it makes me happy.

Vegetable gardening is the real way to save money, and vegetables on the whole do not take long to grow. Indeed, one of the main aims of the grower should be to make his vegetables grow quickly, for grown quickly, pulled or cut young, and cooked immediately, vegetables are tender, succulent, tasty and nutritious.

As already pointed out, you can grow certain vegetables among the flowers or even in a window box, but that way you cannot expect to grow sufficient to supply your needs. It is surprising, however, how much produce can be grown in a tiny plot. Further advice will be found in my companion book, *Vegetable Gardening Made Easy.*

# 8

## CHANGING AN EXISTING GARDEN

When one moves into a new house or a new garden the immediate reaction is to plan changes, to make the place conform to one's own familiar habits and requirements. Yet too often these habits are prejudiced and these requirements irrational. They may have developed out of sheer sloth, a complacent and slipshod acceptance of the results of the passage of time, the comforts of familiarity, the development of taste and personality, and the lack of the element of surprise.

Even more of the same kind of prejudices affect the way we look at our present gardens. In fact often we don't really look at our gardens at all after they have been made and are operating comfortably. Instead of looking at the garden we are looking to see if the grass needs cutting, if that hedge needs trimming, if weeds are growing in that newly dug patch of the vegetable garden. In other words the garden has lost its impact as a unified work of art and has become instead a number of different constituent parts.

One of the most important reasons why gardening can be a pleasure instead of a mere chore is that it can be a creative art, and it can be this only if it is dynamic, growing, changing, showing every evidence of burgeoning life. No garden is ever static and no gardener should ever lay down his spade with a sigh and say, 'That's it. I've finished'. The garden isn't finished; he is. For apart from anything else plants grow, change colour, occupy more space, so that the overall appearance of the garden is never the same from week to week or even from hour to hour.

The enormous popularity of indoor plants should give us a clue to the way we should look at our gardens. Disregard for a moment all talk about indoor plants being a way of furnishing a home, that they bring living green into an artificial world, that they are as beautiful as and longer lasting than cut flowers. Disregard all this and focus your mind on the fact that with indoor plants you look at and care for each plant as an individual, not as a part of a mass. The garden contains so many plants that too often too few retain any individuality. They all merge into 'the border' or 'the rose bed'.

Take a chair out into the garden and set it down where you can sit comfortably and examine a familiar plant, say a group of lupins. Look at the digitate leaves. How many fingers have they? Have they all the same number? Do the plants differ? Are the individual flowers on each spike the same colour? The same size? How are they arranged, in circles, whorls, vertically, horizontally? Are there any seed pods at the base of the flower spike? Are they hairy? Rough or silky?

Give the plant your attention for half an hour and really look closely at it. If you have the energy or the interest take notes of what you see. Next day do it again and see what differences you find. If you are still interested, or if you find surprising changes in this brief passage of time, repeat the observation on the third day. After this you will never be able to look at a lupin again in the same way. You will have established a sort of kinship with it. Lupins will mean more to you than ever they did before, giving you greater pleasure.

It was worthwhile, wasn't it? So what about doing the same thing with other plants in the garden, not only the lovely and dramatic flowering plants but some of the more staid trees such as conifers. You will be astonished at what you see if you look long enough and hard enough and this will once again give you an entirely new interest in and affection for that tree.

Gradually you will build up an acquaintanceship with the plants in your garden and each one of them will begin to mean something to you. Think of going to a party and entering a room full of people all standing about with drinks in their hands chatting to each other. You know none of them yet, so to you this is merely a room full of people. But if you are, say, the hostess, you will know them all and this will not be to you a room full of people, but Bill getting on well with Gloria, Eva looking lovely tonight in that purple dress, Tom growing grey. The people will be individuals, all meaning something special to you.

Once you begin to see the garden as a collection of individual plants you may begin to change your mind about their locations. You may have noticed, for example, that a certain plant has a powerful perfume. Why, then, should it be placed down at the far end of the plot where the perfume is literally wasted on the air? Much better to bring it up near the house so that on summer evenings the scents are wafted on the gentle breeze over friends and neighbours enjoying a casual drink on the terrace. And again, a honeysuckle can look charming climbing up the stump of an old tree, but it will look just as charming on the walls of the house, and from there the perfume will drift in through the bedroom windows. You have noticed that a grey plant stands out beautifully against the dark green background of a neighbour's hedge. Why not go the whole hog and create a silver border there instead of the present mixed and not particularly distinguished medley?

Some ladies become driven by a nesting impulse in the spring when the days begin to lengthen and the sun gradually becomes warmer. They carry out a great spring clean and they move their furniture about into new positions and sometimes they are right and it stays where it has been put and sometimes they are wrong and it quickly gets moved back again. The important thing is that these ladies are expressing their personalities, enjoying their talents as homemakers. Whether they are right or wrong is less important than the fact that they are doing something, not merely sitting back and accepting what lies in front of them.

In a garden it isn't always quite so easy to move the 'furniture' about, and for this reason it is wise perhaps to be quite sure that you are right when you attempt to make a major change. If you yourself have designed the garden and now propose to make some alterations, the probability is that you are right and that the changes you intend to make are the result of considerable thought or possibly changed circumstances. It may be that the children have grown up and left home. It may be that your rheumatism makes gardening less of a pleasure than once it was. You are adapting to circumstances, acting like a rational human being and using your intelligence.

But if you have taken over an already existing garden in a good state of repair but not to your taste, I suggest that you might be advised to live with it for a while before you undertake any major alterations. You may not be able to understand why this feature is placed where it is or why that tree dominates that section of the plot, but if you live with it, preferably through all four seasons, then you will probably come to understand why the previous owner, the creator of the garden, did it his way. You will see that this layout takes greatest advantage of the morning sun and that location for the pool means that it is protected from cold winter winds. Always be prepared to give the benefit of the doubt to any piece of creative gardening or design, remembering that there must have been some reason for doing it that way.

On the other hand there can frequently be a profound clash of interests which insists on an immediate change. Perhaps the previous owner was a rock garden enthusiast and most of the plot is taken up with features which enabled him to enjoy and expand his interests. But you are more interested in trees and shrubs, yet have no space to grow them. Then obviously you must change things radically and at once. Or perhaps the previous owner was a croquet fan and his lawns were laid out as a croquet court, but your own sport is golf and you would prefer to erect a practise net where the hoops once stood. Then change things at once. It's your garden.

Once more, if after accepting and living with a garden design for some time, understanding and appreciating why it was made in this manner, you still think you could improve it aesthetically and practically, then you're the boss: go ahead and change it. No garden is sacred and if you have the time, the energy, and the necessary cash to change things to a pattern more to your own tastes, or more applicable to your own needs, then it is certain that you will get pleasure from doing it. To look out from the house day after day at a garden which grates on your nerves and offends your senses is to suffer quite needlessly, and no matter how great the changes you propose, no matter how much work is involved, you will be right to undertake it for it will give you both peace and pleasure.

There is no virtue, however, in change merely for the sake of change, so be quite certain in your own mind what alterations you intend to make and keep these to a sensible minimum. Because you dislike that clump of shrubs does not mean that they must all go; it might be better merely to thin them out. Because you dislike the position of the tool-shed does not mean that you cannot take advantage of the paved area where it stands. Because you think that the circular bed of scarlet salvias in front of the house is vulgar and tasteless when you move in does not mean that you must do away with the bed entirely, for it might look charming filled with milder, less strident hostas or more emphatic with a dramatic yucca or even covered year round with a carpet of heathers.

So make use of what existing features or plant materials can be fitted comfortably into your own plans and you will cut down the amount of work and money necessary for the changes you wish to make. At the same time have a look around and see if there is a plant over there that would look better over here, see if the paving you remove from the pool area can be used to enlarge the patio. If major work is involved, such as the removal of a mature tree, make quite sure that it must be grubbed out entirely before you set about the task, for it might be that if it were merely cut back it might suit your plans, or perhaps it could be cut down to leave a mere stump which could then have a rose or a clematis growing over it. Ask yourself whether it is necessary to destroy the feature you dislike; cannot it instead be added to, adapted, altered. You find the view of the tool-shed from the house distasteful, and quite rightly so. But instead of taking it down and erecting it in a less obvious position, examine the possibility of planting a weeping ash or something of that nature in front of it, for this would both screen the unattractive building and give you a new decorative feature in the lawn. Or perhaps you could surround it with a screen of beautifully trained cordon fruit trees, which would give you an interest to train and an end product you could enjoy.

One of the problems about most of the creative activities of gardening is that seldom can a single task be carried out on its own. Nearly always in order to do one thing it is first necessary to do another. If you intend, shall we say, to create a labour-saving shrub border in place of the existing herbaceous border, then before you can plant your shrubs you must remove your herbaceous material. And before you remove it from one spot you must decide where you are to put it and prepare that particular site. To destroy that material would be a waste of good living plants. Some of it you may be able to distribute among friends and neighbours. But you cannot just leave it in piles to dry out and spoil – and to get in your way as you carry out the major task in front of you. But the danger in proceeding metho-dically in a sensible step-by-step manner is that you lose interest in your main aim. At first you work at white heat with the ultimate perfection of your new design clearly in your mind, but you get more and more frustrated as you appear to be bogged down in the minor irritations of detail.

For this reason it seems wise if you wish to make gardening a pleasure to concentrate on one task at a time and carry that out as a single operation. Then, when this has been completed to your satisfaction you can turn around and fill in the background work that has needed to be done. In normal British weather clumps of herbaceous plants dug up from one place will come to no harm if they are dumped on bare soil, even on grass, for a week or so. Paving stones can be piled quite neatly in a convenient corner. Tree trimmings can be burnt and tree trunks converted to logs.

Get on with the task which interests you and leave the remainder to be done at a later stage. If this book has one message it is that to make gardening a pleasure it is necessary to rid it of anything that might frustrate or impede you in what it is you wish to do. In my own case, one border I made and loved became more and more of a burden because the farm weeds which encroached from the land on the other side of the nearby hedge made it a constant battle to keep clean. Throughout the years the trees planted, fairly well spaced, had grown well enough to be seen as individuals, and so one day a family conference was held and an agreement was reached that we should do away with that border and take the lawn up through and around the trees to the hedge. The improvement is enormous. And reluctant though I was to lose the border, the garden has gained a new perspective and I have found a way of relieving myself of a great deal of uncreative work.

This brings me to a further matter to be considered when changing an existing garden, whether it is one that was originally made by someone else or whether it is one which you made and with which you have lived for many years. There is an opinion that once a major plant, usually a tree, has been put in position it will grow in that place for ever. It is true that some trees and shrubs will outlive us and continue attractive to the end of their days. But many beautiful flowering trees and shrubs which we buy and use today are cultivars, cultivated varieties bred for the exceptional beauty of their flowers, their foliage or their fruits and with little attention paid to longevity. Many are beautiful only when they are young. As they grow older they lose their freshness and attraction and ought to go, to be replaced by something more exciting and worthy of garden space. Mere sentiment shouldn't hold us back.

If you decide that you would like to replace, say, a flowering cherry with another flowering cherry, then it might be wise to choose another site, not necessarily at the other end of the garden, but just far enough away to prevent any possibility of soil sickness from affecting the new resident. This is particularly so with roses. After growing roses for some years in any particular spot it is always a good idea to move the bed completely and to allow the original rose bed to be covered with grass or to bear some plant material other that the original crop of roses.

The fresh soil will certainly be appreciated by your roses, in spite of the fact that you might have cultivated and fertilized the old site with the greatest of care and attention while the bushes were growing there for all those years. Sometimes you will find that you can make a major change of this nature in a simple way by extending the bed on one side while you grass it over at the other. We have done this ourselves with considerable success.

Whenever any changes of this nature are made it is always worth while to give the vacated soil a little attention. Fork in a lavish layer of peat, compost, or some similar humus-making material together with a good handful of a long lasting fertilizer to every square yard (1m²), for this will enrich and reactivate the soil which has held its crop for long enough to deplete the supplies of natural goodness it normally bears.

If the area on which you are working is one which has previously been paved or covered in some other manner so that neither sun nor air could get to it, then take special pains to bring back the soil into good heart. It is almost certain to be sour and unproductive and will need plenty of light and air as well as the health-giving attention of humus-making materials. It is best to dig soil of this nature as deeply as is convenient for you and to leave it roughly dug so that the sun and air, the rain and the frost, can penetrate the depths and give it new life. If it is near the house and you fear that it will be an eyesore for the summer, broadcast seed of some flower which will flourish on poor soil, shirley poppies for example. They will give a splendid show for a season. You could also try a crop of potatoes.

Happily, gardening is a two-way activity, and in exactly the same way that it is possible to restore a sour, sick, and unhappy soil to new and productive life, so the garden and your work in it can affect you, can bring you health and happiness. To make gardening a pleasure is to gain a double advantage.

# INDEX

# Scented Border

(Dianthus - Hardy.)

Gaultheria Procumbens.
　　　　(Red Berries) Aromatic.

~~Ground~~ Ground Cover.

Ceanothus "Gloire de Versailles"
　　　　(Blue Flowers)

Ceonothus. "Thyrsiflorus Repens"
　　　　Blue Flowers

X Osmarea Burkwoodii.

Osmanthus Delavayi. (Holly leaves)
　　　　　　　　　　　Spreading.

Viburnum X Juddii. Hardy.
　　　　　　　　(White Flowers)

Honeysuckle, Early & Late.

Sweetpeas - Evensong.

Variagated Sage.

Skimmia.

(Tubs) - Flowering Shrubs.

　　　Malus Everests.
　　　(Pink/white Blossom)

( Sulphate of Ammonia
= High Nitrogen Total
4 oz Growmore per sq yd